Praise for Free to Parent Workbook

"I've led parenting groups for years and 'Free to Parent' has been the best book I've ever used, hand's down. The wisdom and practical advice that Ellen and Erin give are priceless. 'Free to Parent' encourages a heart connection with our children that not only gives us hope of a real, lasting relationship with our kids, but also one that will help guide our children to live lives honoring to God. The companion workbook offers great discussion questions that truly allow for deep thought, conversation, and honest growth. I recommend these books with all my heart."

—Susan Sprouse

"I was the mom who would parent my heart out all day long and then stuff my nose in a parenting book until I fell asleep late at night—always searching for a new set of rules or a spiritual formula that would answer all my parenting questions so I could be the perfect parent raising perfect children. And I was tired. Jesus doesn't approach us with rules and regulations. He comes near us with love and truth. In the same way, Ellen Schuknecht and Erin MacPherson respectfully and vulnerably offer themselves through their stories and strategies that address our hearts, giving us permission to loosen our white-knuckled grip on life and allow the Holy Spirit to not only liberate us, but also our beloved children. With this book and workbook, we can indeed learn to be 'free to parent.' "

—Molly Ingram

" 'Free to Parent' is an absolute necessity for parents who understand the power of the gospel and are seeking to parent their children in a manner that is synergistic with the love and grace of Jesus and His Good News. This book has challenged me as a mother to closely examine my true intentions in the moment, allowing for transformation where my heart has become more aligned with the goal of establishing loving connection and trust in my relationships with my children, rather than control. I highly recommend 'Free to Parent' and its companion workbook; they served as a catalyst of significant growth in my parenting journey!"

—Laura Jennings

Free to Parent Workbook

Ten Weeks of Deep Study to Help You Escape Parenting Traps and Liberate Your Child's Spirit

Ellen M Schuknecht
with
Erin M MacPherson

Family Wings, LLC
www.familywings.org
Austin, TX

© 2015 by Ellen Schuknecht

Published by Family Wings, LLC
www.familywings.org
Austin, TX 78652

Printed in the United States of America

All rights reserved. No part of this publication may be reproduced, stored in a retrieval system, or transmitted in any form or by any means—for example, electronic, photocopy, audio recording—without the prior written permission of the publisher. The only exception is brief quotations in printed reviews.

Library of Congress Cataloging-in-Publication Data is on file at the Library of Congress, Washington, DC.

ISBN: 1515186814
ISBN: 978-1515186816

Scripture quotations are from the Holy Bible, English Standard Version, copyright ©2001 by Crossway Bibles.

To protect the privacy of those who have shared their stories with the authors, some details and names have been changed.

DEDICATION

To my precious grandchildren:

Josiah, Kate, Jude, Hadassah, Greta, William, Isaac, Asa, Elsie, Alma, and Bethlehem

Contents

Acknowledgements ix
Introduction xi

Session 1: Replace You with Him 1

Session 2: Replace Obedience with Desire 10

Session 3: Replace Discipline with Discipleship 20

Session 4: Replace Control with Connection 28

Session 5: Replace Complacency with Growth 38

Session 6: Replace Lectures with Love 49

Session 7: Replace Anger with Forgiveness 60

Session 8: Replace Grumbling with Gratitude 72

Session 9: Replace Distractedness with Rest 84

Session 10: Replace Hopelessness with Hope 95

Endnotes 106

Acknowledgements

Writing a book as a mother-daughter team has been a joyous and tender process, one that has united our hearts and woven together stories from both generations. I am very grateful to my oldest daughter, Erin MacPherson, whose insights and suggestions have been vital in the development of this workbook. I am so very proud of my daughter who is able to take my rambling ideas and weave them together into a manuscript that makes sense. Thank you Erin, for your patience with me, for your willingness to teach me how to organize my thoughts, for your courage to be honest with me, and for your perseverance in sticking with me along the way.

I want to also like to thank my dear friend Laurie Sibley, who has painstakingly copyedited every page, offering up her thoughts and insights with a generous spirit and open heart. You are a gift from God and minister to me in ways I can't even put into words.

I want to also express my gratitude to Susan Sprouse who, along with Laurie Sibley, is a member of the Family Ministry Team at Veritas Academy. Susan led a group of Veritas parents through this workbook in draft form, which provided valuable feedback and insight into the development of final version.

I also wish to thank the entire Family Ministry Team and the parents from Veritas Academy who have already journeyed through the chapters in this workbook. Their encouragement and support kept me going.

I would also like to thank the following people for their insights, support, and encouragement without which this workbook would not have been written:

To my husband Glen, who patiently has waited for me to come out of "the cave," a term he uses for the home office where I write.

To my grandchildren who provide many great stories to illustrates our points.

To my other children, Troy & Stevi Schuknecht and Peter & Alisa Dusan, who give wise counsel and encouragement along the way.

And to my many friends who shared stories and suggestions, providing depth and wisdom to this workbook.

I am deeply grateful for every person who has made this workbook a reality.

Introduction

My grandchildren have built a "secret" fort out of sticks and brush on our property that adults are not allowed to enter. Inside their secret lair, they have created a make-believe world, which currently takes place in colonial times. They go off on "hunts" and have family spats and even contemplate their feelings towards the American Revolution. It's their world, where they are free to play on their own terms, outside of the watchful eyes of their parents.

Halfway across the country, we moved my 87-year-old mom into a delightful senior living facility last year. She loves the amenities—meals, activities, even friends, but she still longs to be back in her home. She wishes to live wholly on her terms and hates having her freedom restricted.

To be free is a deep call on the hearts of both the young and the old. And everyone in between. In Galatians 5:1a we read that it's *"for freedom Christ has set us free."* What does it mean for us to "live" set free?

For my grandkids and my mom, freedom means their right to be and do as they please, to be their own boss. Freedom in Christ, however, means the willingness to allow Him to be in control of one's life as the means to victory.

This freedom results in an inner contentment with who we are in Christ.

Why is it so difficult, particularly in our roles as parents, to live in the joy and freedom that Christ offers? Because we love our children more than life itself and we want them to thrive so badly that the very idea of handing our precious kids over to Jesus feels terrifying.

So what do we do?

We tend to parent out of default—either as we were parented or in direct opposition. Default sets in habits and ways of doing things that simply may not work. Yet we keep on keeping on because it is all we know how to do—and think we are supposed to do.

Throughout my years of working with families, I see the very same core issues ensnare parents—and then kids. The devil really isn't that tricky. He takes good sounding ideas and uses them to trap us, with traps such as self-sufficiency, legalism, or perfectionism to take us off course to God's best.

The end result is Christian homes tainted by anger, defeat, and discouragement.

I believe that Christ came to set us free from the chains we place around our own hearts. Finding freedom as a parent is what *Free to Parent* is about and this companion workbook takes each chapter deeper. My prayer is that through deeper study, your joy as a parent will also grow deeper as you become free of the common traps parents find themselves in.

Only at the feet of Jesus do I have a clearer picture of who I am as a parent and who my children are to become as adults. Only at the feet of Jesus am I consistently able to parent out of a peaceful heart. Only then do I operate in the freedom of the Lord and not from the confines of human reasoning. Apart from Jesus, I lose my way.

I pray that this workbook helps you contemplate the little things so that you can be free in the big things. Because with that freedom, comes the ability for you to be the parent that God created you to be.

Ellen

Session 1

REPLACE YOU WITH HIM

Begin this session by reading chapter 1 in *Free to Parent*.

As you read in *Free to Parent*, when I graduated from college and got engaged at the age of 21, I was armed with Psychology and Teaching degrees that focused on Child Development and Family Relationships. I was determined to establish a Christian family—different from the one I experienced growing up. I was going to do it right. I was going to be a super wife and mom. Confident in the head knowledge I possessed, I taught parenting classes before our first child was born. In addition, I began to write a book by infusing ideas from my college courses, with the Christian principles I was now learning.

But God blessed us with three spirited, driven kids with minds of their own. And not a single one of them responded to my carefully crafted methods and strategies as I had envisioned they would. Soon life, as a mother of three young children, took over and the rough beginnings of my book were stuffed into a box in the corner of my closet. (They were hidden somewhere in my attic, and perhaps someday I will pull them out and get a good laugh!)

Isn't it wonderful how God grows us in ways that we would never expect? For me, he grew me by giving me kids who pushed the boundaries of what I thought I already knew, and in doing so, challenged me to not only think deeply, but to lean on Him. Likewise, I am confident that God is teaching you through your parenthood—and in the process, he is helping you to draw closer to Him.

This session is about how to replace "you with Him"—contemplating how we can allow Him to not only become the center of our parenting decisions, but how we as parents can learn to trust Him implicitly both for our kids' lives and for our own.

Replacing me with Him: Parenting out of a surrendered heart

As Christians, we know that God calls us to surrender—*to replace our own interests, wants, and hopes with an all-consuming desire for Him.* To guide our children to this place, we must get to a place of surrender ourselves. And to get there, we must allow Christ to set us free from deceptive ideas about ourselves. Here are a few ways that I've been able to do that.

Break free from false ideas about self-worth

Many of today's young parents were raised during the "self-esteem movement" of the '70s and '80s. Now as parents, these adults strive to nurture their kid's self-esteem at any cost. Are we as a culture making flawed decisions based on that aim?

I think so. In a modern online dictionary, self-esteem is defined as "a favorable impression of oneself."[1] Which means kids are taught to accept, understand, and value themselves "just because." In my mind, the next logical conclusion after "I am great just the way I am," is "I'm great so why do I need a Savior?" It's a slippery slope. The Bible also says that we were each created in His image and thus our body is a temple. We must teach our kids to respect themselves, like themselves, to value themselves, and to stand up for themselves, but we also have to teach them to break free from false ideas about self-worth. Because when that happens, God is merely someone to help us get the desires of our hearts rather than the sovereign God of the

Bible who tells me how He desires and thus determines how I should live.

Ponder Philippians 2:3 and what it has to say about self-esteem: "Let nothing be done through selfish ambition or conceit, but in lowliness of mind let each esteem others better than himself." How can we as parents help our kids to find balance between necessary self-respect and overblown self-esteem?

_____

_____

_____

_____

Break free from self-sufficiency

I can always know that I am beginning to lean on my own self instead of on Him when my prayer life falls off. Rather than making prayer a priority, I start to focus primarily on making my own plans and find myself devising all sorts of clever strategies to manage my decisions and those of my family members.

This is a natural tendency for all of us. I think we have all heard (and probably even said!) that "God helps those who help themselves." While there is a measure of truth in this saying, there is also a measure of error. We should be diligent workers and responsible for ourselves, but the deception lies in a moralistic aim to be self-sufficient and independent. When we start to depend on ourselves, we slowly start to believe ourselves responsible for our own successes, failures, and even our worth in Christ.

That's not the Gospel of Christ! In fact, the Gospel message is more like "God helps those who recognize that they are unable to help themselves." The pathway to abundant life, to freedom and joy, is not by way of self-sufficiency and independence; rather it is by becoming dependent upon an all-sufficient God whose living water never runs dry.

Consider John 15:5: "I am the vine; you are the branches. Whoever abides in me and I in him, he it is that bears much fruit, for apart from Me you can do nothing." What does this tell you about times when you begin to lean on yourself rather than on Him?

_____
_____
_____
_____

Oswald Chambers said this: "Jesus writes a new name in those places in our lives where He has erased our pride and self-sufficiency and self interest. Some of us have the new names written in spots only—like sanctified measles." [2]

Are there any matters in your life that you need to take out of your own hands and place in His?

_____
_____
_____
_____

How can we raise responsible kids who both know how to solve their own problems, yet also see their deep need of God?

_____
_____
_____
_____

Break free from your worldly identity

As my children grew, I began to find my worth based on my identity as a super mom. I had thrown myself fully into motherhood and while that may not sound like such a bad idea, I struggled to see life apart from my kids. My children had filled a huge place in my heart for so many years. And as I found myself in an empty nest, I found myself sinking into a mire of depression.

What would fill my heart now? After much prayer and contemplation, I realized that **my kids had not merely been my primary focus, but they had also become my meaning and purpose in life.** My empty nest left me with a crisis of identity. It was in this season of life, that I began to earnestly pursue God. My deep feeling of emptiness caused me out of desperation to seek God's fullness. An insatiable hunger grew in me to pursue Him.

In my "nothingness" I desired His "everything-ness." Suddenly I understood what Andrew Murray meant in *Absolute Surrender* when he said, "If I am something, then God is not everything, but when I become nothing, God can become all, and the everlasting God in Christ can reveal Himself fully." [3] This empty point in my life marked a huge turning point in my intimacy with God.

I only wish I had realized how to surrender my fear and worry much sooner so that I could have raised my own children with a free heart, and with an identity fully founded in Him.

What empty seasons in your life have proven to be turning points in your journey with God?

_____

_____

_____

_____

How do you struggle to find your identity in Christ and Christ alone? What people or things trigger you to find your identity—even if momentarily—in something other than Him?

_____

_____

_____

_____

GROUP STUDY SECTION

The Beatitudes: Cultivating a desire to give it all to Him

A few years ago I decided to memorize the Sermon on the Mount. Doing so was certainly a challenge but one that pressed the inherent truths deeper into my heart. As I began to write *Free to Parent*, I was elated to discover that the Beatitudes lined up seamlessly with the themes I had outlined for the book.

The Beatitudes describe the disposition of the heart—or attitudes—out of which virtuous actions rise. The foundation is found in the very first one, namely being "poor in spirit." Unless we grasp this, the remainder can remain unattainable. Yet it's so tempting to ignore this aim, especially as we train up our children.

Many (okay, probably all) kids from go through a crisis of identity and a crisis of faith at some point in their childhood. This is usually in pre-adolescence, but can show up earlier or later, and in some kids it can show up multiple times. They become dissatisfied with just about everything. With themselves. With their family. With friends and school. Even with God. They don't like how they feel on the inside but aren't so sure they want to give Jesus entrance to change them. All this angst is wrapped up in one messy package that scares parents to death!

This is a crucial point in our kids' lives where heart decisions are made and direction is established. Many are tired of pretending to be the "awesome, nearly perfect child" their parents claim them to be. Others grow ashamed realizing that the hidden person within does not line up with who their parents desperately want them to be. Some give up trying to be "good enough" and others rebel entirely. This is the time when learning what it means to be "poor in spirit" can be a balm to their hearts. "Perhaps there is a way out of this mess I feel on the inside." In order to grow a virtuous heart, we must all first come to the place where we stand empty before the Lord and ready for Him to define and shape us.

The First Beatitude: Seeing My Need for Jesus

*"Blessed are the poor in spirit,
for theirs is the kingdom of heaven."*
Matthew 5:3

To be "poor in spirit" does not mean an admission of insignificance. Nor is it about devaluing oneself. Rather it's a confession "that I really do need Jesus!" To be "poor in spirit" is where we each begin with God, with empty hands humbly admitting our shortcomings. It's coming to grips with who we are NOT, rather than justifying who we are, making room in our hearts for Jesus to create in us a new identity with a pure heart. Perhaps, we as parents would not stress so much when we see our "flesh" come through if we fully understood that "flesh" is not redeemable without the redemptive work of Christ. Then our children would be more likely to open up to us and to God, rather than suppressing what is really going on in their hearts.

Discussion questions

1. What does "poor in spirit" mean? Give an example of someone you know who is "poor in spirit" and explain why you chose that person.

2. How can we teach our kids to be "poor in spirit"? What are some actions that demonstrate this trait?

3. How is your own attitude reflective of being "poor in spirit"? Are there times when you struggle with this just like your kids do?

4. How do we balance an appropriate measure of "self-esteem" with a desire for our kids to be "poor in spirit"?

I pray that each of you finds freedom in the Lord to parent your kids by His leading and that you set your hearts free from deceptive traps taking you off course. Here is the scripture passage for this session to meditate on:

Jeremiah 17:5-8

⁵ Thus says the LORD:
"Cursed is the man who trusts in man
and makes flesh his strength,
whose heart turns away from the LORD.
⁶ He is like a shrub in the desert,
and shall not see any good come.
He shall dwell in the parched places of the wilderness,
in an uninhabited salt land.
⁷ Blessed is the man who trusts in the LORD,
whose trust is the LORD.
⁸ He is like a tree planted by water,
that sends out its roots by the stream,
and does not fear when heat comes,
for its leaves remain green,
and is not anxious in the year of drought,
for it does not cease to bear fruit."

Session 2

REPLACE OBEDIENCE WITH DESIRE

Begin this session by reading chapter 2 in *Free to Parent*.

A short while ago, I flew to my nephew's wedding in Colorado along with my three adult children and five of my grandchildren. We had a fabulous time! Three days staying in an adorable ski chalet in the Colorado mountains coupled by great food, great company, and a beautiful wedding had us all cheerful...until it came time to go home.

We didn't make the wisest of plans for our return trip to Austin. After a five-hour car ride from the wedding venue to Denver, we arrived at our hotel at 2 AM. With an early flight and still a 20-minute ride to the airport, we left the hotel 2½ hours later at 4:30 AM, only to find a collision jamming up the freeway. Pulling up to the airport with a very short window of time remaining, we sent two adults to return the rental cars while the rest of us clamored out of the car with piles of luggage and car seats. That left me with pregnant, nauseous Alisa and five cranky kids, ages 1, 3, 5, 6, and 8 lugging everything into the airport to begin the check-in process.

We must have been quite the sight!

Breathlessly, I turned to eight-year-old Joey and directed him to help carry bags. He glared at me, crossed his arms in defiance and shouted, "I am too tired."

"Can't you see that we are all frustrated?" I barked back at him. I started to chastise him, to tell him why he had to obey, but bit my tongue. Because I know that no one wins in a "try-and-make-me" power struggle. And with sobbing four-year-old Greta in one hand, and weeping one-year-old Alma in the other, I knew that none of us could take a showdown at that moment.

I prayed. And the answer came like a wave: I asked Hadassah and Kate to cart more than their share and calmly told Joey to "at least stand out of the way." Out of the corner of my eye, I watched Joey's face soften. He blinked a few times, swallowed hard and then grabbed two large rolling suitcases and piled his belongings on top of them. In a matter of seconds, he transformed from an argumentative fit thrower to a helpful young man. Even more, he later told me that he genuinely felt badly, and that he was motivated to change directions. Incidentally, we all made our flight but without a minute to spare.

All of us—yes, even adults—have moments when our own selfish desires don't align with the desire God has for us. This session will be talking about aligning those desires to God's so that we can raise children who truly desire Him.

Replacing obedience with desire: Parenting our kids so they desire God

Each of us comes into the world with a heart orientation toward selfish desires. Our *want to*'s don't naturally line up with *ought to*'s. In the story above, Joey's *want to* was to rest. His *ought to* was to help. And had I gotten into a battle with him over his selfish desires, he would perhaps have learned that doing what he wanted would result in punishment, but he wouldn't have learned about desiring right.

Break free from consequence-driven parenting

Many parents take verses such as *"Children, obey your parents in the Lord, for this is right."* (Ephesians 6:1) and *"If you love Me, you will keep My commandments."* (John 14:15) to mean that by demanding "first-time obedience," we are teaching our kids to be holy. But I feel like by demanding obedience from our kids, we miss something deeper and more vital. We never address the very motivations within that drive our children to obey or disobey.

Jesus doesn't give up on any of us when we fail to respond the first time to the quiet nudging of the Holy Spirit. Instead, He graciously grants each of us opportunities to get up and try again. And again. And again. While consequences still occur, and doors may even close because of my disobedience, His Spirit does not leave me nor forsake me but gently moves me along a path of growth towards a heart that desires Him.

This isn't an easy task! It's actually fairly simple to dole out consequences in response to our children's behavior, but it's much more difficult to speak to the desires of their hearts. But what an aim that is! Imagine a generation of kids who, instead of following a list of rules or should's, innately desire God's will in their hearts.

Consider the concept of "first-time obedience." Why does it sound so appealing? In what ways does it fall short of how Jesus disciples us?

_____
_____
_____
_____

What are some ways you can speak into the desires that motivate your kids' hearts?

_____

_____

_____

_____

Think of a time that you gave your child a consequence for wrongdoing. Consider how you could have effectively spoken to your child's desires as part of that situation?

_____

_____

_____

_____

Break free from "compliant" and "strong-willed" labels

Does anyone here have a so-called strong-willed child? The child that seems to want to assert his or her will at every turn, who always finds a way to push the limits, to run across that line in the sand and have a party? Many of us do, and while I think it's essential for parents of so-called strong-willed children to seek methods and strategies to deal with these children, I also think it's essential for them to push aside that label. And start thinking about their children as children of our King—flawed, yet beautiful children who God is molding to fit into His plan.

Here's why: Getting certain children to obey is relatively easy. My second-born son was what you would consider a "compliant" child. He generally followed the rules and did what we asked of him. God created these children with a desire to please and because of this, so-called compliant kids are obedient and respectful. Many parents come to see such a child as "naturally good." I think this is as big of a mistake as labeling the "strong-willed" child as "difficult."

It says in the Bible that each of us is born with an innate sin nature. Which means that all kids—"compliant" or "strong-willed"—have hearts that desire their own *wants* instead of God's will. This innate desire is obvious in certain kids. But in others, it's not as obvious. Interestingly, the challenge for authentic heart change may be steeper in the long run with a child who has been labeled "good" or "compliant" and doesn't really sense any need of change.

This paragraph from *Free to Parent* is worth repeating:

> It's easy to be deceived by well-behaved kids, who have learned to look clean on the outside but still remain dirty on the inside. They then grow up into young adults who are accustomed to pretending and see no need for internal transformation. They get along just fine, getting what they want without all the pain of examining their own hearts. And that's exactly what we promote when outward obedience is the highest aim within the Christian family; individuals who can serve God in outward ways, yet bluntly disobey Him by failing to deal with anger, greed, lust, pride, and bitterness in their hearts. [4]

Consider your own kids. Which would you label "compliant" and which "strong-willed"?

_____

_____

_____

_____

Have you ever considered the fact that it could actually be easier to parent your "strong-willed" kids than your "compliant" kids? Does this ring true to you?

_____

_____

_____

_____

How could this idea change the way you respond to your kids individually? How will you respond differently to your "strong-willed" kids? To your "compliant" ones?

_____

_____

_____

_____

Break free from "head obedience"

God created each of us with deep desires. Some of these desires enhance our lives and make us feel alive and fully human. But others can be a destructive force, like a tornado, plowing down everything in its path. Rightly ordered desires will produce rightly ordered lives. Wrongly ordered desires will bring about disordered lives.

As parents, we can force obedience through strict consequences, but we cannot order the desires of their hearts. Our kids have to do that themselves, and when we put all of our emphasis on their outward behavior, we often lesson our ability to connect with their hearts.

Think about some of the "good" desires that God has given each of your kids. How are those desires being used to enhance that child's life? How could those desires be used to help that child grow closer to God?

_____
_____
_____
_____

What desires do you recognize in your children that need to be adjusted to move them in a positive direction?

_____
_____
_____
_____

GROUP STUDY SECTION

The Beatitudes: Cultivating a desire for repentance

This past summer, Hadassah, my five-year-old granddaughter chose to be baptized. All week long, she had looked forward to the event, as her parents answered her questions and explained its significance. She woke up that Sunday morning however worried and agitated and asked her daddy, "what if I am sometimes still naughty after I am baptized?"

That is a good question, without pretense, from a young girl who knows her own tendency to misbehave. Last month Hadassah chose to be disruptive in her kindergarten classroom and when questioned afterwards by her mom, she simply said, "It was fun." Her willingness to be honest and examine her own heart is something to encourage. When children learn to examine their own hearts, rather than focus on what is going on around them, they come to comprehend not only the consequences of their good and bad choices, but also what drives their choices to begin with.

Often a child simply does not recognize his own motivations. Just like us! It takes practice to gain insights into one's own heart and a heart that is pure will grow out of an awareness that, without Jesus, our human nature is prone towards selfishness.

As kids grow older, and as kids learn to examine their lives, they will discover that their self-centered pursuits do not produce the happiness they crave. Kids, who learn to desire right, learn early in their lives that only pleasing God brings about true contentment and helps them to fulfill their true purpose.

A practice of honest self-evaluation will render kids (and adults) more willing to move from viewing God as someone who will help them live as they want, to someone who leads them to live as He desires. A heart that loves what is good will come to seek good

> ## The Second Beatitude: True Repentance
>
> *"Blessed are those who mourn,*
> *for they shall be comforted."*
> **Matthew 5:4**
>
> To recognize my own selfish nature is not enough. To truly repent, mourning is necessary which renders me able to receive the comfort of the Lord and become free from selfish desires. *"For godly grief produces a repentance that leads to salvation without regret, whereas worldly grief produces death"* (2 Corinthians 7:10).
>
> We must guide our children to walk through repentance, and not lessen the grieving process, so that they can receive the comfort of the Lord. Kids who back away from repentance, and hide what is going on in their hearts, lose sight of the gospel message and begin to choose instead the desires of the world. And that's when the destructive presence of shame further blinds them to the truth.

Discussion questions

1. Four steps to cultivating a heart that desires God are: self-examination, ownership, prayer, and repentance. How do you (or can you) teach your kids to practice these on a regular basis?

2. What problems do your children cause that you tend to take ownership for? How could you hand these issues back to them?

3. Do you find yourself wanting to excuse your child's wrong doing and rationalize it away? By attempting to ease their sense of guilt, could you be standing in the way of heart change?

4. What is one area where you feel like your child struggles with a desire to follow Christ? What are you doing or could you do to change that?

I pray that as your kids grow, you find the freedom to stop controlling them and instead help them cultivate a desire for God. Here is the scripture passage for this session to meditate on:

Psalm 51:6-12

^{6} Behold, you delight in truth in the inward being,
and you teach me wisdom in the secret heart.
^{7} Purge me with hyssop, and I shall be clean;
wash me, and I shall be whiter than snow.
^{8} Let me hear joy and gladness;
let the bones that you have broken rejoice.
^{9} Hide your face from my sins,
and blot out all my iniquities.
^{10} Create in me a clean heart, O God,
and renew a right spirit within me.
^{11} Cast me not away from your presence,
and take not your Holy Spirit from me.
^{12} Restore to me the joy of your salvation,
and uphold me with a willing spirit.

Session 3

REPLACE DISCIPLINE WITH DISCIPLESHIP

Begin this session by reading chapter 3 in *Free to Parent*.

My parents responded in anger when they didn't like how I behaved. I remember one time I dropped a bowl and it broke across the kitchen floor. My dad exploded, yelling at me, and I was honestly frightened he was going to hurt me. That was the way things were in my household.

When I became a mom, I found myself responding in the same manner at times with my own kids. I would later feel deep regret over my anger and purpose not to let anger get the best of me time and time again. At the same time, I was bent on making my kids obey. They were going to be obedient children, not just because it was right, but also because I considered their obedience my success as a parent. So when they did not obey, I felt like a failure and that anger boiled up.

Here's the thing: Anger actually works to make kids obey. It's frightening, and out of fear, many children will behave in order to avoid it. But what I often missed as an adult is that while anger can keep behavior in check, it also shuts down the heart connection we need with our kids.

I am convinced that in order for us to truly discipline our kids, we have to disciple them. And in order to disciple them, we must connect with them. And that is why I would like to focus this session on how we can connect deeply with our kids even as they misbehave and cause us to feel angry.

Replacing discipline with discipleship: Parenting our kids so they connect with God

Every child will disobey, and every parent will respond in anger. It's how we handle that disobedience...and that anger...that will change our kids from the inside. As you work through the following pages, I want you to consider your reactions to your kid's misbehavior and contemplate how you could respond in a way that inspires connection rather than distance.

Break free from assuming intent

Oftentimes as parents, we assume that when our kids misbehave they are being defiant, controlling, or manipulative. Anger bubbles up as we assume they are being *bad* and doing the wrong thing. I often hear parents say things like "he seems to want to press my buttons" or "the more rules I put on him, the more he wants to break them, seemingly to get me mad."

I understand this feeling—trust me, I've been there, but I also have come to believe that our kid's misbehavior is so much more than pure defiance. In fact, I believe that often it's an emotional reaction to feeling misunderstood or frustrated. For example, a child who is playing a video game and is asked to turn it off and come to dinner may throw the controller or start to whine. Is the child being defiant and choosing to play the video game instead of come to dinner against your wishes? Maybe. But more likely, the child is disappointed that he has to turn off the game and frustrated that game time is over and responding emotionally.

This doesn't mean he shouldn't put down the controller and come to dinner by any means, but as his parent, an awareness of the issue would help you to respond correctly. You could walk over and hug him and say something like: "I understand it's frustrating when you are doing something and have to stop. But if you throw the controller, it's going to break and you won't have a video console anymore. What can we do to make sure you don't react in frustration again?"

Think about a time your child disobeyed you. Did you stop to contemplate the reason? If so, what reason did you assign as his or her intent? Is it possible you misinterpreted his or her intent?

_____
_____
_____
_____

Consider the idea that kids' misbehavior is often a result of them being unable to clearly express their frustration rather than defiance. Does this ring true to you? How does it change the way you will discipline your kids?

_____
_____
_____
_____

Does your level of frustration ever influence your own actions? What strategies do you use to overcome that? Could any of those strategies be taught to your kids?

_____
_____
_____
_____

Break free from anger

I still remember the day I quit justifying my angry responses, which I had for years blamed on the disobedience of my kids. I recognized it as sin in my own heart and asked the Lord to take away this bent towards anger. Slowly, He did and began to teach me a gentler way. I still have to address anger from time to time, but it's rare now, and I know how to rid my heart of it before it bubbles out. Jesus changed me within so that my natural inclination is no longer one of anger.

Anger hurt my relationship with Erin for many years and it took time to repair our connection. But today, Erin and her family live next door to us and we have a very healthy relationship. If you struggle with getting angry at your children, don't give up or assume that your mistakes have ruined your relationship with your kids forever. No child is born into a perfect family. No parent is free of mistakes. But it's never too late to change. Just participating in this study is a first step, and I want to encourage you to spend the coming months examining your own heart and freeing yourself from the perceptions that not only bind you but also blind you to a gentler way.

Consider these verses about anger:

> *"Know this, my beloved brothers: let every person be quick to hear, slow to speak, slow to anger; for the anger of man does not produce the righteousness of God"* (James 1:19-20).

"A fool gives full vent to his spirit, but a wise man quietly holds it back" (Proverbs 29:11).

How do these words inspire you to change the way you discipline your children?

_____

_____

_____

_____

What are some ways you could express authentic anger over disobedience without responding in anger?

_____

_____

_____

_____

Break free from punishment

At times, I have felt very ashamed at my lack of patience and self-control when I parented my children. Slowly, it began to dawn on me however, that part of the issue was that my views on discipline were keeping me trapped in a destructive cycle. Once I gained a grander view of discipline (broader than just behavior management) and along with it developed an eternal perspective of the aim of discipline, my methods began to expand beyond the limits of my human inclinations to more of a spiritual perspective.

How we view discipline and what we aim to accomplish by it, plays a significant role in keeping our children both reachable and teachable. If we think of discipline as punishment or simply doling out consequences for bad behavior, we lose so much of the deeper things God wants us to give them.

Punishment is about external control. It involves us handing down a penalty for our kid's misbehavior. "I am in control and decide how to punish you when you don't behave properly." Discipleship however is about influencing your child to gain an inner sense of control.

Punishment is also fear based, often with a harsh, angry flavor. It's a bogus power we grab on to when we fear losing control over our kids and focus on managing behavior rather than influencing it. It's about threats and demands in an attempt to gain obedience. Discipleship, on the other hand, is about teaching and training, the transfer of influence from one heart to another. Discipleship flows out of a loving, connected relationship, and while punishment may lead to outward compliance, I believe that only discipleship leads to sincere obedience.

Have you ever felt like discipline doesn't work for certain kids? How could this idea of discipleship vs. punishment be helpful with these children?

_____

_____

_____

_____

For a specific misbehavior, what are some ways you could use discipleship vs. punishment?

_____

_____

_____

_____

GROUP STUDY SECTION

Cultivating a desire for gentleness

A mother came to me at school telling me she had told her adolescent daughter that she would not be allowed on their computer for a year. Her daughter had violated the rules and while she regretted the overly harsh disciplinary action, she felt she needed to stand firm on her word and not back down. I suggested that she should back down, and explain to her daughter that she had made a hasty decision in a moment of anger and now she desires to establish a plan by which her daughter can actually earn her trust back.

I am very grateful that God is a God of second chances. Consider Rahab, a harlot, who later married into the lineage of Jesus. Or Peter, who denied Jesus three times and was chosen to be the rock upon which the church would be built. Or King David. The list goes on and on of Biblical figures who, after committing serious mistakes, went on to become notable heroes of faith.

It's easy to make grandiose statements with our kids like "I will never let you drive my car again." or "that's the last time you are inviting a friend over to spend the night." But kids need chances relatively soon to prove they can learn to do things differently. They need opportunities to get up and try again so that failures don't take hold and define them. Mistakes are only failures if they prevent a person from getting up and trying again.

My husband and I dropped the practice of grounding our kids. We found that it trapped us into a plan of action that kept us in a position of management and control while our kids grew frustrated and distant in the process. Instead, we offered up plans that expressed our belief in their ability learn. We instead told them that they would be given a chance to try again once we felt up to trusting them again. It was our responsibility to hold high standards and their responsibility to figure out how to live by them. This approach gave us flexibility and gave our kids the opportunity to earn our trust again.

Discussion questions

1. What are you doing that keeps your kids reachable and teachable? What are you doing that pushes them away and makes them defensive?

2. Do you consider yourself as more tender or more tough? What about your spouse?

3. Has there been a time recently when you have misunderstood your child's intent and given a consequence inappropriately? What could you do in the future to avoid this?

4. What things do you do that frustrate your kids? How can you help them to deal with the frustration so they don't get to the point of exacerbation or disobedience?

I pray that as your kids grow, you find the freedom to hold in your anger and allow your kids the space to grow. Here is the scripture passage for this session to meditate on:

---

1 Corinthians 4:14-21

[14] I do not write these things to make you ashamed, but to admonish you as my beloved children. [15] For though you have countless guides in Christ, you do not have many fathers. For I became your father in Christ Jesus through the gospel. [16] I urge you, then, be imitators of me. [17] That is why I sent you Timothy, my beloved and faithful child in the Lord, to remind you of my ways in Christ, as I teach them everywhere in every church. [18] Some are arrogant, as though I were not coming to you. [19] But I will come to you soon, if the Lord wills, and I will find out not the talk of these arrogant people but their power. [20] For the kingdom of God does not consist in talk but in power. [21] What do you wish? Shall I come to you with a rod, or with love in a spirit of gentleness?

Session 4

REPLACE CONTROL WITH CONNECTION

Begin this session by reading chapter 4 in *Free to Parent*.

A number of my grandchildren are spirited kids who can be challenging at times. Three-year-old William shares the top spot with this honor. "Will-I-Am" he proudly states and he is rightly named. Trying to control Will rarely results in him behaving the way his parents desire. Instead, his strength of character and resolve rise to the surface in monumental ways.

During the school year, Tuesdays are set aside for being with my grandchildren. All but three-year-old Will are students at Veritas Academy, a University-Model School, in which students are in class every other day and then do a full day's load of school work at home on the alternate days. When I first began to help out in this way, I was overly focused on controlling the process—of getting the work done efficiently before it was too late in the day. This "make it happen" mindset was met with resistance by all of them—including Will. He was not about to be controlled—and certainly not ignored—while the others had work to do. The more I tried to control the tempo and the outcomes of the day, and the more I clamped down on Will, the more frustrated we all became and the longer the process actually took.

Then it dawned on me that Will just wanted to be a part of the school experience, to connect with the others and with me even though he was too young to have actual assigned work. So I began to intentionally include him in the school day, to make plans for him as well. It took a bit more planning and even felt like a distraction from what I was supposed to be doing, but by allowing him to connect meaningfully in the school day it took away his need to get attention in negative ways.

Now when the others read quietly, he curls up on a couch with the devotional *Jesus Calling* and pretends to read as well. Each Tuesday, he chooses the same book, which he stores in his Opa's coffee table. He is united with the experience by "reading" alongside the others—not a child's book with pictures but what he sees as a "chapter book" so he can be like his big brother. "I read about Jesus," he tells me proudly.

Now, when the others are working on a written assignment, Will is writing "sentences" and when the others are working in their science notebooks, he is making projects of his own. Someday his scribbles will form words but for now it's enough to just be connected in the process with the rest of us. He labors over projects with scissors, glue, paper, and markers making creations to bring home to his mom. He listens to his sibling's lessons and gives his answers to questions along with them. The best part is that his siblings no longer see him as a distraction but enjoy his presence and love hearing his contributions to the discussions as well. (They are learning not to laugh!) Rather than shooing him away, they are welcoming him into the process.

Replacing control with connection: Parenting our kids from a place of connection

When we consider our primary responsibility as parents to be that of protecting our children from hardship and conflict, we grow compelled to navigate for them any hardships that come as well. In the process our connection with who they are and what they really need is broken down and therefore our influence as well.

Break free from intervening

Troy, our son, was timid and reserved as a child. Unlike his sisters, he rarely threw fits. He was an easy child who demanded little from us. But he lacked assertiveness. I remember watching him play soccer as a six-year-old on a rather large team. During breaks, many of his teammates would wave their arms wildly in front of the coach asking for playing time. Troy, on the other hand, stood at the back of the mob, quietly and shyly raising his hand. The coach did not notice because his attention would be drawn to the boisterous demands of others. Troy lost out on playing time for a while, not because the coach had anything against him, but simply because he was not seen. As a mom, I felt angry on my son's behalf. And sad. I was tempted to talk to the coach, to set things right for my son. But I was married to a coach and Glen encouraged me to take a different approach. Rather than attempting to control the circumstances, Glen suggested that we begin to teach Troy how to respectfully assert himself. As we began to guide Troy in this way, we discovered that he had been trying not to be demanding, like some of his teammates, but he also didn't know how to stand up for himself. As we considered how to guide Troy, based on how he was wired, we were then able to influence him to grow stronger for himself. As he learned how to advocate for himself, his playing time increased as a result of his own efforts.

List ways you find yourself wanting to ensure that your kids don't experience even mild disappointment or discomfort as well as times you feel compelled to wipe out their sadness and disappointment.

_____

_____

_____

Then ponder how to whittle down your list of what you regard as necessary to intervene in. When we try to prevent our kids from experiencing anything less than comfortable, we are also preventing them from learning the skills they need in order to deal with difficulties when they do come. And they will! Especially when the going is rough, kids need to learn to govern themselves, to figure things out on their own, and to make wise decisions. Rather than swooping in too quickly, do your kids a big service and focus on helping them develop these skills, which are vital for growth and success.

Ask yourself if your attempts to control rise out of need to alleviate your own anxieties—that by doing so you can somehow control the outcomes and prevent bad things from happening. How has it worked out for you and your child when you have intervened too much?

_____

_____

_____

_____

Break free from hyper-vigilant parenting

As mentioned earlier, sometimes we simply try too hard to make things work out on behalf of our kids. One of my friends truly desires for her kids to do well in school so she double checks her kids' assignments over and over and works with them to complete the problems to ensure their success. Notice I said success, not understanding. It backfired. A few months ago her son Tim came home with a low grade on a math test. Having grown overly dependent on his mom's efforts, he found himself unable to be successful without her. Her well-meaning efforts had backfired.

If there is a common trap Christian parents fall into, it's control. In an effort to get desired behavior or outcomes, these parents often resort to efforts to control both their kids and their circumstances in order to make things happen well for them. From over helping with school projects and assignments to intervening in attempts to resolve social issues, it's easy to step in and take over because we deeply want things to go well for our kids. Yet our efforts to control can actually hamper their own development of self-control.

Kids need lots of practice in learning problem-solving skills and in making wise decisions in order to gain confidence in their own abilities. This is the only way to develop grit—a characteristic that describes successful people. That's why we need to often remind ourselves to *stand back rather than step in*. From the sidelines we can express empathetic understanding for what our child is struggling with and offer guidance. Empathy and understanding are tools that build connection. Stepping in often breaks it down because it is perceived as control. What we desire for good can backfire.

When do you find yourself wanting to swoop in and intervene with your kids? Think about times when intervening in this way has stood in the way of allowing them to develop some muscle on their own.

_____

_____

_____

_____

Do you try to protect your children from failure before giving them space and time to struggle through things on their own? Consider in which ways you can offer empathetic guidance instead.

_____

_____

_____

_____

Think of a time when your vigilant parenting hurt authentic connection with your child?

_____

_____

_____

_____

Break free from engaging in struggles for power

An argument with Joey, my nine-year-old grandson, rarely results in one of his parents "winning." Joey loves to engage his parents into arguments and he devises all sorts of ways to trap them into arguing. Whether it's over food or who's at fault (his favorite), he is wired to argue. Yet doing so usually makes everyone dirty in the process.

Any time you ask your child to do something and he refuses to comply—you're in a struggle for who is in control. When this push for control escalates into an argument, you are in a power struggle. Even though it feels like "losing" at the moment, the best approach at this point is to drop your end of the rope. It's less about giving in and more about refusing to participate in a ugly pattern of behavior right then, in order to engage in a constructive manner later, when it's possible to do so. Kids are masters at designing power struggles you really can't win, like "try to make me care" or "try to make me try" or "try to make me eat." Trying to come out on top in one of these struggles is a recipe for failure.

However, nothing ensures a power struggle like your child's belief that he can't talk to you reasonably about something. Fight the urge to lecture or criticize and invite your child to talk to you about it later when tempers have cooled down. Connect with your kids' needs to assert themselves by listening intently to what they have to say and then guiding them to use effective strategies for dealing with conflict instead.

What triggers your child to try to hook you into a power struggle? What triggers you to engage?

_____

_____

_____

_____

GROUP STUDY SECTION

The Beatitudes: Learning to connect with our kids' hearts

Glen and I struggled with communication from the very beginning of our marriage. He grew up in a home where showing emotions was considered weak and he was criticized often for how he felt. He had no idea how to respond to his emotional wife. All he knew was to be analytical and critical of me in the process. I learned to keep my feelings hidden and he learned to not ask how I felt. We both resorted to maintaining a safe distance from each other, instead of working towards a close connection, and a wall grew between our hearts.

It was the constant, yet gentle, prodding of the Holy Spirit, and the fear of failing our own kids, that caused us both to make some deliberate choices a few years down the road. We both concluded that regardless of how we individually perceived things to be, *we would purpose to* move towards each other, which meant we had to be honest about what was really going on in our hearts, and allow each other to be honest as well. We had to become a safe place for each other.

Prior to this, we had erroneously assumed that all of our arguments and discussions needed to end in agreement. That meant, one of us would come out the winner and the other the loser. One of us would have the control and one of us wouldn't. What we discovered, however, is that authentic communication does not require agreement—*just a willingness to understand each other*. This was a huge key in opening the doors of our hearts to each other. Once we put aside trying to determine who was right and who was wrong, and focused on understanding instead, a safe connection began to form and our conversations grew authentic and heartfelt.

Isn't that how it is with our kids? If efforts to share their thoughts with us result in criticism, correction, and control, they will quit communicating except to tell us what they think we want to hear. When we focus more on listening and trying to understand what they are thinking and feeling, kids feel assured of being heard, and become much more receptive to correction and to change. "I hear your heart and will try to understand how you feel" opens the door to receiving what you are to say because the safety in being understood has been established.

Meekness is about a gentle steadfastness—standing on what is right and true but not being forceful or harsh in demanding it. When Paul reminded the Thessalonians of his ministry to them, he said in 1 Thessalonians 2:7, *"But we were gentle among you, like a nursing mother taking care of her own children."* Meekness allows us to be a safe place to land for our children yet holds to standards at the same time.

The Third Beatitude: Strength Under Control

*"Blessed are the meek,
for they shall inherit the earth."*
Matthew 5:5

When a parent is strong, but overbearing, the child is likely to disconnect out of fear. At the same time, a child will not find security when strength is absent. "Strength under control" however paves the way for healthy connection between parent and child.

A meek spirit within makes me safer to connect with. This word, in Greek, embodies a strength that is properly controlled and covered in humility. In the ancient Greek culture, the meek person was not passive and weak—rather a person with self-controlled strength.

Discussion questions

1. In which ways can you build in times of meaningful connection with each child?

2. Do you find yourself wanting to correct your kids when they share what's on their hearts? Consider one way you can change that will serve to foster a closer connection with your kids as they age.

3. In Matthew 11:29 Jesus said, *"Take my yoke upon you, and learn from me, for I am gentle and lowly in heart, and you will find rest for your souls."* Why would a gentle approach with our kids make them more willing to learn from us?

4. What circumstances tempt you to resort to force or manipulation in dealing with your kids instead?

5. What emotions rise to the surface in you when you feel forced or manipulated into doing something?

6. How specifically can you model more meekness in your parenting?

I pray that as parents you learn how to be safe and secure places for your kids to land. I pray that God will teach you to listen more and control less, to truly know your children as individuals, and to understand them at a heart level. Here is this session's scripture passage to meditate on:

James 3:13

Who is wise and understanding among you?
By his good conduct let him show his works in the meekness of wisdom.

Session 5

REPLACE COMPLACENCY WITH GROWTH

Begin this session by reading chapter 5 in *Free to Parent*.

Back in 2003, my husband and I drove across the country in our U-Haul to begin a new life in Texas. I had just completed six years as the head administrator of a start up school in Oregon and while I wasn't quite ready to retire from working altogether, I was not about to get involved in the demanding work of another new school. I longed to be free of the pressure and looked forward to having little to worry about except fun things like what kind of cookies to bake with my future grandkids. After years of raising kids, the idea of kicking back sounded very appealing.

But God had something different in mind for me: Growth.

Within a couple of years of our move, He placed me right back working in a brand new school, this time in a school with a new model, a new strategy, and even greater pressure than the first one. There were many days that I fell to my knees and told God this wasn't what I had wanted or planned. But looking back, I can see that God had better things in mind for me than a life of ease. And in the past ten years, I've learned to experience the sweetness of surrender in the face of major challenge, and to find contentment in the inherent discomfort of growth.

God gave me this life phase to continue to refine me, to grow me, to use me. And while it hasn't been easy, it has certainly been life changing. I know (yes, from experience) that God chooses to grow us at the times that we least expect it, and through means that we would never imagine. With that in mind, I'd like to focus this session on how we can not only allow God to use our circumstances to grow us, but how we can help our children as God does the same with them.

Replacing complacency with growth: Parenting our kids so they grow into the men and women God wants them to be

We are all always growing—but in what direction? There are periods in my life where I look back and see that I was growing closer to God, closer to family, closer to the life God planned for me. But I also see times where I was growing in complacency, in selfishness, away from the very things that God had so blessed me with. It's a lifelong struggle for all of us—and there will naturally be similar times for our kids when they grow in the completely wrong direction. But with some simple tools—and a lot of prayer—we can help our kids stay on a continuous trajectory of growth.

Break free from the wrong trajectory

Do you ever look at your kids and wonder what exactly they are doing? I have! I remember a long period when my oldest daughter was in college when I wondered if her sole intention in making the choices she did was to drive me insane! But now, I see how God used those experiences—even the tough ones—to refine her. In 1 Peter 1:7, God says that our faith is tested and purified by the fire, and while those experiences aren't always fun, they are what help our kids become who God wants them to be.

What about you? What challenges in your life are causing you to grow in ways you had not imagined? As you look back on your life, what experiences stand out as milestones of growth? Why?

_____

_____

_____

_____

Break free from fear

We introduce our kids to Jesus. We want to see them grow up with godly character and we envision launching our teens into the world as committed believers and responsible adults. Yet many adolescents wind up stuck in the transition, so much so that a newly classified life stage is now being defined for 18-25 year olds. Many stall in these years, with no clear direction in life and remain strangely unmotivated to achieve independence. They prefer instead to be taken care of. Why this complacency and lack of direction? An entire book could be dedicated to this one topic but I will highlight a few tendencies that lead to this transitional pause that can last for years before many adolescents finally grow up into adulthood. Fear drives many parental decisions. Yet fear can, and often does, hold kids back. While safety is a wise aim, keeping our kids safe must not overshadow the development of life skills so that our kids can GROW UP into adults with the ability to navigate the world and also to have something to offer. Consider the following quote by Christine Gross-Loh, author of *Parenting Without Borders: Surprising Lessons Parents Around the World Can Teach Us:*

> Ellen Hansen Sandseter, a Norwegian researcher at Queen Maud University in Norway, has found in her research that the relaxed approach to risk-taking and safety actually keeps our kids safer by honing their judgment about what they're capable of. Children are drawn to the things we parents fear: high places,

water, wandering far away, dangerous sharp tools. Our instinct is to keep them safe by childproofing their lives. But "the most important safety protection you can give a child", Sandseter explained, "is to let them take...risks." Consider the facts to back up her assertion, Sweden, where children are given this kind of ample freedom to explore, has the lowest rates of child injury in the world.[5]

What frightens you? What fears do your kids currently have that prevent growth?

_____

_____

_____

_____

If you have read anything about Finland lately, you are likely aware of its excellent reputation with regard to education. Having been raised by Finnish immigrants, with many relatives still living in Finland, my "insider" perspective is that their success has less to do with having great schools, however, and more to do with the culture of the Finnish homes. Beginning at an early age, kids are expected to learn essential life skills, to help around the house and learn a work ethic and even make important decisions. Go into a Finnish knife store, something Finns are known for, and you will find a whole section of knives designed for little hands because young Finnish kids are expected to learn how to use tools we have come to consider dangerous. In addition, both boys and girls learn how to cook, clean, do laundry, yard work, fish, hunt, work with all sorts of materials ranging from wood and metal to fabric and yarns. Gaining expertise grows confidence and opens the door to opportunities and growth. After visiting with relatives in Finland this past summer, I returned home with a stronger passion to teach my grandkids practical skills both for inside and outside the home. (And packed in my suitcase were two knives for our oldest grandsons so that they can learn to whittle with wood.)

If your child would be graduating from high school today, what life skills would you want to make sure he or she had? Is fear holding you back from teaching any of these skills?

_____
_____
_____
_____

Break free from perfectionism

Our youngest daughter, Alisa, gave early indications that she was an overachieving perfectionist. She would grow frustrated and crumple her artwork each time it did not look just right and she would throw her homework into the trash when she made a mistake. She certainly was not the stereo-typical youngest child, competing fiercely even with her older siblings. With her own peers, only the highest outcomes were acceptable in any endeavor she chose to participate in.

Our concerns were buried within the delight we found in her achievements. What parent doesn't enjoy success with their children? In time, however, we began to see signs of deep-seated anxiety. As soon as she reached one goal, her joy would be short lived, and she would soon begin to drive herself to still a higher goal. The issue was not with the goals she set, however. Kids need to set high aims. The problem was that she based her worth entirely on whether she reached these lofty goals.

Alisa's response to a perfectionistic spirit is different from kids with a perfectionistic bent who respond instead by setting low aims because the risk of not reaching their goals is too terrifying even to try. Their "I don't care" guise hides their deep fear of failure and discouragement. In addition, they are prone to procrastinate which further hampers growth and gives them a handy reason why outcomes are less than desired.

Whether your child is an overachieving or an underachieving perfectionist, the issue of perfectionism needs to be addressed. When performance is the end all and be all, the process of growth will not hold up. Growth will falter, even for the overachiever, at some point.

What indicators of perfectionism do you see in yourself? In your kids?

_____

_____

_____

After her freshman year as a Longhorn swimmer, in which she reached All-American status, Alisa's growth as a swimmer faltered when she came down with mononucleosis. No matter how hard she tried, her body would not perform. Still she swam (no excuses for the overachiever!) her entire sophomore year, and as a result, the illness returned in double force. She was in her worst nightmare: on a swim scholarship but unable to carry out her team's expectations. God used what mattered most to Alisa—high-pressured swimming at the University of Texas—to move her identity in performance to one rooted in Him.

I thank her coach to this day for telling Alisa "swimming does not define you. It is merely going back and forth in the water." This woman, a repeat Olympic gold medalist heading up an elite swim program, illustrated grace to Alisa, breaking down the misconceived image she held of herself. What a life-changing message Alisa gained through this difficult season, when God used "failure" in the natural to bring about victory in her spirit. Although her body was still recovering, she swam very well in her senior year because anxiety did not weigh her down. The fear of failure was no longer present because she had experienced what she considered to be failure and got through it. The two-year illness put an end to her lifelong dream of swimming in the Olympics but it paved the way for more important growth to be realized within.

Break free from a fixed mindset

Consider the following statement by Salman Khan in his blog titled *Why I'll Never Tell My Son He's Smart:*

> My 5-year-old son has just started reading. Every night, we lie on his bed and he reads a short book to me. Inevitably, he'll hit a word that he has trouble with: last night the word was "gratefully." He eventually got it after a fairly painful minute. He then said, "Dad, aren't you glad how I struggled with that word? I think I could feel my brain growing." I smiled: my son was now verbalizing the telltale signs of a "growth mindset." But this wasn't by accident. Recently, I put into practice research I had been reading about for the past few years: I decided to praise my son not when he succeeded at things he was already good at, but when he persevered with things that he found difficult. I stressed to him that by struggling, your brain grows. Between the deep body of research on the field of learning mindsets and this personal experience with my son, I am more convinced than ever that mindsets toward learning could matter more than anything else we teach. [6]

The research Kahn refers to is largely that of Dr. Carol Dweck, who has been studying people's mindsets towards growth and learning for decades. (I strongly recommend her book *Mindset: The New Psychology of Success*.) The discoveries are exciting and center on the discovery that our intelligence is not fixed. Rather it grows when we embrace tasks where we might struggle and fail.

Dweck states that people who erroneously see their intelligences as unchangeable have a fixed mindset while people with a growth mindset rightly believe that their capabilities can grown by effort and struggle. Therefore they embrace challenges because they understand that effort and tenacity change the outcomes.[7]

What weaknesses in yourself do you fear? Does this fear hold you back from doing something you wish to do? What weaknesses in your kids do you fear?

_____

_____

_____

_____

Group Study Section

The Beatitudes: Cultivating a desire for spiritual growth

Peter Dusan was not exactly the sort of young man I desired my youngest daughter to date in high school. Something about this young man intrigued me, however. I think it was his zeal. What Peter wanted, he pursued with diligence. But that meant that as a popular, outgoing, high school athlete, he pursued partying with more diligence than anything else. Alisa on the other hand, preferred to spend time with a small circle of friends from her youth group and swim team and was adamant about not dating in high school. At all. She claimed to want nothing to do with Peter and turned him down. Despite that, I sensed that she was actually interested in him. There was something about Peter—his zeal, his vibrancy—that drew people towards him.

Prior to Peter's sudden interest in Alisa, in September of 1998, Peter had stepped into a student-led Bible study, taking place over the lunch hour in my husband's math classroom. Invited by a classmate, he entered the room more out of curiosity than out of personal interest, to see what the "nerdy" Christians were up to. That day the call of God fell on Peter who found himself weeping on the floor, unable to shake a deep-seated change taking place within. Peter responded fervently to God's call on his life and began a surprising transformation from a party guy to a high school evangelist. Within days, he started carrying a Bible with him everywhere, eagerly digesting its pages and sharing what he learned with others. Peter's reputation expanded with him as he began to talk a new language and walk a new walk and pursue a different set of friends. Old friends waited for him to return to his previous ways, assuming he would tire of this new life but it never happened.

Almost eight years later, in May of 2006, Peter and Alisa got married. His pursuit of her never wavered although the years certainly included conflict between the two. His walk has definitely not been without potholes either, but Jesus transformed him into a man

Alisa is blessed to call her husband and we are honored to have as our son-in-law.

Peter's diligent *pursuit* of Jesus continues to fuel his growth in all areas and it defines him. It's true for all of us; what we diligently pursue, we will grow zealous about and what we diligently pursue will define who we are. Only as we know Him will we come to be more like Him. *"Those who seek me diligently will find me"* (Proverbs 8:17b).

The Fourth Beatitude: Spiritual Growth

"Blessed are those who hunger and thirst for righteousness, for they shall be satisfied."
Matthew 5:6

The people in Jesus' day knew what it meant to be hungry and thirsty. They experienced this as a part of life. Just as hungering for food and thirsting for water are signs of physical health, a longing after righteousness is a driving force that signals spiritual health. What we pursue with desperation, we will find and it will come to define us. May it be the Lord Jesus Christ that we are desperate for because without Him we will lose our way.

Discussion questions

1. *"The soul of the sluggard craves and gets nothing, while the soul of the diligent is richly supplied."* (Proverbs 13:4). What are you zealous about? What do you diligently pursue?

2. What about your kids?

3. What we pursue we grow to love. What worthy pursuits are you encouraging your kids to engage in?

4. What we grow in we find satisfaction in. In which ways are you growing spiritually? In which ways are your kids growing spiritually?

I pray that each of your children grow in the knowledge of who God is and who He has designed them to be. Here is the scripture passage for this session to meditate on:

> **2 Peter 1:5-8**
>
> *[5] For this very reason, make every effort to supplement your faith with virtue, and virtue with knowledge, [6] and knowledge with self-control, and self-control with steadfastness, and steadfastness with godliness, [7] and godliness with brotherly affection, and brotherly affection with love. [8] For if these qualities are yours and are increasing, they keep you from being ineffective or unfruitful in the knowledge of our Lord Jesus Christ.*

Session 6

REPLACE LECTURES WITH LOVE

Start this session by reading chapter 6 in *Free to Parent*.

As you may have gathered by now, my childhood was full of disconnected relationships. My father was aloof and rarely affirming. His law practice and farm consumed most of his emotions and energy. My mom was busy managing not only a house and five kids, but also helping dad with our orchards, gardens, and cattle. Neither Mom nor Dad expressed much interest in our lives; and they rarely expressed delight in us. Their way of showing love was to work hard at provision, and while that was important, their inability to connect with our hearts left us feeling as if our deepest human needs were unattended.

Not too long ago, I read the book *Escape the Lie* by Walker Moore. While reading, I made the connection between the style of relationships I grew up in and what for years has felt like a shadow covering my heart. The author wrote about what he calls an "orphan heart," one that feels abandoned or rejected, and somehow outside of God's redeeming love. Because no one is raised by perfect parents, we all can struggle with some elements of an "orphan heart." None of these strongholds need remain however, if we understand the depth and breadth and length of our heavenly Father's love. Until we do, we are prone to a driving need to prove our worth in every circumstance.

As a missionary, Mr. Moore has worked with true orphans who live in orphanages around the globe. He found that no matter how loving the interactions, the orphans tended to avoid close relationships rather than enjoy the kindness and love that came their way. One worker said, "we take care of these children, we love them—and they want to hurt us. They lie. They steal little items whenever they can. They mock our value and undermine our authority. They think the whole world is against them so they must fight for their rights. No matter how much love we show them, it's never enough." [8]

An orphaned heart arrives at the conclusion that "I alone must take care of myself." An orphan heart trusts his or her deepest needs to no one—not even God. This realization brings new meaning to Jesus saying, *"I will not leave you as orphans"* (John 14:18a).

Without Christ, we are all orphans. But we as parents can help our children to escape the "orphan heart" not by being the most perfect, most loving, most flawless parents we can be, but instead by trying to show God's perfect love to our kids with everything we do. This session will discuss how our words and actions can lead our children straight to the perfect, all-accepting love of the One who will never leave us orphaned.

Replacing lectures with love: Parenting our kids while overflowing with God's compassion and grace

We all have an "orphan heart" in one way or another—I know I still struggle with some of these wounds. And as parents, there is nothing we can do to help our kids completely escape the feelings of hopelessness, abandonment, discouragement, or desperation, but we can point them directly toward our Heavenly Father who is the only One who can, in fact, heal every wound and right every wrong.

Break free from your own orphan heart

Awhile back, one of my friends came to my house and sat down at my kitchen table and started to cry. She sobbed that she was trying so hard to guide her kids to Jesus—to help them to see what they needed and how to have an intimate relationship with Jesus and while they were doing great, she felt like she was failing. She had mentioned this to a mentor of hers and her mentor had told her that she would never be able to lead her own kids to Jesus unless she had her own life in order first.

Now, I want to be clear that I disagree with this in many ways—God uses each of us with all of our imperfections for his glory. And we can certainly make an impact on our kids and on our communities even when we still have our own messes to deal with. That said, as parents, one of the best ways we can help our kids to truly see God's love is to embrace it ourselves.

Here are a few descriptions that could indicate you have an orphan heart:

- Do you find yourself striving for acceptance?
- Do you look in the mirror and find fault with what you see?
- Do you need to keep certain things about yourself hidden?
- Do you find it difficult to rest?
- Do you desire intimacy but can't seem to get it?
- Do you struggle when a loved one points out a fault in you?
- Do you believe no one will take care of you but yourself?
- Do you sense God to be distant?
- Do you feel as if you have a barrier keeping you on the outside looking in?

Which, if any, ring true for you?

_____

_____

_____

_____

What practical steps could you take this week to give those struggles to God and start moving past them?

_____

_____

_____

_____

Break free from a false understanding of love

God's Word has life changing power. Know what the scriptures say about love and apply them to the circumstances you and your family face each day. Share with your children the truths you discover about God's love and establish them as principles for your family to live by. Here are four to consider for your list:

1. **God's love is sacrificial and not self-serving.** How difficult it must be for the parents who lost their sons to beheading by ISIS terrorists. I can't begin to imagine their pain. Then I think of God who chose to sacrifice His Son for us. I wonder what depth of pain He felt, watching His son be crucified. Yet, He chose this out of love for us. Let's never tired of teaching our kids about John 3:16: *"For God so loved the world that He gave His only Son, that whoever believes in Him should not perish but have eternal life."*

   In turn, the love He asks us to extend is sacrificial in nature, not focused on what we want but on what others need. *"Do nothing from selfish ambition or conceit, but in humility count others more significant than yourselves. Let each of you look not only to his own interests, but also to the interests of others"* (Philippians 2:3-4).

2. **God's love is for mankind as a whole and at the same time, personally for each of us.** Mankind matters to God.

Regardless of where in this big wide world we are born, each person is equal in His sight. Children need to gain a sense of this unity with children everywhere who are all precious in His sight. At the same time, we are created and loved as unique individuals. So speak vision and unique purpose to your children, something God will reveal to you as their anointed authority. And help them see how their unique gifting can be used to spread God's love to others.

3. **God's love delights in each of us.** Flying home from Oregon one time this year, I sat beside a mom and her 12-year-old daughter. I immediately sensed a strong bond between the two of them. They talked and laughed and looked fondly at each other. This mom delighted in her daughter. I was touched by their sweet exchange of words and never once in the entire flight did I hear any harshness—only a loving conversation between a mom and her adolescent daughter.

   Your sons and daughters need to know how precious they are in your eyes and how precious they are in the eyes of God. Let them know that the Lord takes pleasure in His people (Psalm 149:4) and even His reproof is out of delight for His children (Proverbs 3:12). They don't benefit from flattery or excessive praise but they benefit deeply from knowing that you enjoy spending time with them, that you value who they are, and believe in who they are becoming. Determine to express delight in your children regularly so that they would not feel the need to find this elsewhere.

4. **God's perfect love casts out all fear.** To know that God loves me allows me to lean upon His arms in times of need. This alone takes away my fear. To know that God loves my children moves me to pray for them steadfastly rather than fret and worry over them. Spend more time praying for your children than fretting over them!

"There is no fear in love, but perfect love casts out fear. For fear has to do with punishment, and whoever fears has not been perfected in love" (1 John 4:18).

"Do not be anxious about anything, but in everything by prayer and supplication with thanksgiving let your requests be made known to God" (Philippians 4:6).

What are some specific ways you are teaching your kids to love sacrificially?

_____

_____

_____

_____

Take time to consider the words in Psalm 139 (included at the end of this chapter) and jot down some phrases that reflect God's love for you as an individual.

_____

_____

_____

_____

List three ways you could express delight in your children. Set a goal to do all three in the coming week.

_____

_____

_____

_____

Break free from what love is not

While human relationships bring me security and comfort, and the love of others buoys my spirit, it's God's love that brings me victory. The more confidently I walk in His love, the stronger my steps become, regardless of where my path takes me. Nothing need defeat us when we are secure in His love, which surpasses our weaknesses. The love of God frees us from bondage within and allows us step into an "Abba Father" relationship and enjoy His presence.

As parents, we are most effective in showing God's love to our children when we come to see ourselves, not as orphans, but as His inheritance. Knowing God will never abandon anyone of His children, because He loves us personally, removes the shadow of the orphan heart. Certain ways we habitually parent our kids may seem loving at the time but turn out more destructive in the end. Here are a few things that love is NOT:

1. **Giving people what they think they need to be happy.** Learning to be content with what they have is a far greater aim than striving to get what they want whenever they want it. Give them what they really need by learning to say NO when it's the wiser choice. It can feel so unloving at the time to hold to firm boundaries, but your kids will gain much from wise boundaries and in hindsight will even grow to appreciate them.

2. **Making others the center of our lives.** The demands of others—yes, even your kids, should not run your life. In fact, being at someone's "beck and call" raises kids who become very self-focused. They then grow angry when their requests are not immediately addressed. Teach your kids how to serve others rather than expecting others to serve them.

3. **Giving generous doses of flattery and praise**. Flattery and excessive praise have nothing to do with love, although saying such things feels loving at the time. Expect them to han-

dle reality and give them plenty of loving encouragement to grow and improve. Security comes in knowing "mom values me even though I am not that great at soccer right now." Anxiety grows, however, when mom comes to a game and sees that "I am not the best on the team, like she thinks I am."

Which "love is not" is most challenging for you as a parent? Why?

_____
_____
_____
_____

Do you feel loved when you are flattered and praised? Why or why not? What are some alternatives that would be more effective?

_____
_____
_____
_____

GROUP STUDY SECTION

Cultivating the deepest love you can give your kids

My cousin died suddenly last year from a massive heart attack. He had just retired and was building a retirement home with his wife. Now she is left to complete the tasks and move ahead alone. Although we spent time together as children, like most of my dad's extended family, family connections on his side were not maintained. I haven't seen my cousin in over twenty years and I know little about him. I wonder if he knew Jesus. Did anyone love him enough to be the light of the gospel for him?

The most important way to love your kids is to point them to the love of Jesus. Tell them regularly about His love for them. Let them see love in action in your life and tell them of the great things God has done in your own heart. When they see your life rooted and grounded in Him, when they see your strength and your peace coming from Him, when they sense the ultimate joy that comes by way of a surrendered life, they will more likely be drawn to Him.

Discussion questions

1. What truth about God's love is most poignant for you at your current life phase? Why?

2. Is there a "love is not" area that you struggle with? How can you overcome it as you parent your kids?

3. What human relationships do you delight in? How can you show your delight while still depending on God's love only?

4. What is one way that God shows love that is especially difficult for you? How can you help your family to focus on that area this year?

I pray that as your family learns more about God's love that both you and your kids learn to love like God does. Here is the scripture passage for this session to meditate on:

Psalm 139

^{1} O LORD, you have searched me and known me!
^{2} You know when I sit down and when I rise up;
    you discern my thoughts from afar.
^{3} You search out my path and my lying down
    and are acquainted with all my ways.
^{4} Even before a word is on my tongue,
    behold, O LORD, you know it altogether.
^{5} You hem me in, behind and before
    and lay your hand upon me.
^{6} Such knowledge is too wonderful for me;
    it is high; I cannot attain it.

^{7} Where shall I go from your Spirit?
Or where shall I flee from your presence?
^{8} If I ascend to heaven, you are there!
If I make my bed in Sheol, you are there!
^{9} If I take the wings of the morning
and dwell in the uttermost parts of the sea,
^{10} even there your hand shall lead me,
    and your right hand shall hold me.
^{11} If I say, 'Surely the darkness shall cover me,
    and the light about me be night,'
^{12} even the darkness is not dark to you;
    the night is bright as the day,
    for darkness is as light with you.

¹³ *For you formed my inward parts;*
you knitted me together in my mother's womb.
¹⁴ *I praise you, for I am fearfully and wonderfully made.*
Wonderful are your works;
my soul knows it very well.
¹⁵ *My frame was not hidden from you,*
when I was being made in secret,
intricately woven in the depths of the earth.
¹⁶ *Your eyes saw my unformed substance;*
in your book were written, every one of them,
the days that were formed for me,
when as yet there was none of them.

¹⁷ *How precious to me are your thoughts, O God!*
How vast is the sum of them!
¹⁸ *If I would count them, they are more than the sand.*
I awake, and I am still with you.

¹⁹ *Oh that you would slay the wicked, O God!*
O men of blood, depart from me!
²⁰ *They speak against you with malicious intent;*
your enemies take your name in vain.
²¹ *Do I not hate those who hate you, O LORD?*
And do I not loathe those who rise up against you?
²² *I hate them with complete hatred;*
I count them my enemies.

²³ *Search me, O God, and know my heart!*
Try me and know my thoughts!
²⁴ *And see if there be any grievous way in me,*
and lead me in the way everlasting!

Session 7

REPLACE ANGER WITH FORGIVENESS

Begin this session by reading chapter 7 in *Free to Parent*.

My two-year-old granddaughter Alma is very...let's call her spirited. A few days ago, my daughter Alisa caught her walking around the house with a full cereal bowl and milk, taking bites as she walked across their carpet and sat on furniture.

"Alma, we eat breakfast at the table. You can choose to sit in your high chair or on a stool," Alisa calmly requested.

"No want it!" Alma screamed.

"If you don't choose, I will choose for you."

"No want it!" Alisa knows that Alma's temper flares when things don't go her way so she quickly swooped in and took the cereal away lest she have a full bowl of cereal thrown across her living room.

If we're being honest, Alma's actions are pretty normal for a two-year-old. She was born with a propensity to demand her way and become angry when she doesn't get it. That anger can result in fighting, arguing, cruelty, strife, vengeance, disrespect, and bitterness. And while most of us adults have learned to stifle these reactions, anger can be a snare for all of us. In Proverbs 22:24-25 we are warned to *"make no friendship with a man given to anger, nor go with a wrathful man, lest you learn his ways and entangle yourself in a snare."*

Anger is part of the human experience. We can't avoid it or get rid of it. We can, however, learn to respond to it with grace and forgiveness.

Forgiveness is one of our highest humans needs. Without genuine forgiveness, there can be no security in our relationships—either with God or with others. And without security, we are unable to draw near to those we need the most, especially when we struggle. The act of extending as well as receiving forgiveness is a foundational building block of growth and the habits we develop early on often come to define us as adults. When the practices of forgiveness are not established in a home, what takes their place tends to ensnare and blind us and anger fills up the void.

Replacing anger with forgiveness: Parenting our kids so they are able to forgive

Anger is good. There are many instances in the Bible where God feels anger and His just anger is what invokes righteousness and justice time and time again. Oftentimes, kids are taught to either stifle their anger or explode in their anger and these reactions are not only unhealthy, but are far from the holy way that God displayed his emotion of anger. By teaching our kids to respond in the way that Jesus does to anger, we can teach our kids how to forgive easily and respond gracefully in any situation.

Break free from the tendency to be conditional in extending forgiveness

Jane (the person I describe in chapter 7 of *Free to Parent*) has disengaged herself from all of her siblings, as well as her first husband, and now even her oldest son. Not long ago I attended his destination wedding, and have to admit that part of me found a measure of satisfaction that I was invited to the wedding and she wasn't. *It served her right*, I rationalized silently, *based on her offenses against her son and my family.* I began to realize, however, that this mindset was a clear indicator that I had not fully forgiven her.

Having recently read the Old Testament account of Jonah, I found myself relating to his feelings. Jonah was mad when God changed his mind and wanted to extend grace to the Ninivites. He felt they were deserving of God's wrath and he had a personal reason to feel that way. He wanted to see God wipe out the city because the Ninivites had committed horrendous acts against his country and the people he knew. He wanted them to get what they deserved. The last thing he felt like doing was taking the long trek to this hostile city to tell them of God's love and forgiveness. He did not want God's grace to be extended to the very people who had destroyed many of his own kin. I began to see my own lack of compassion in not desiring God's grace to be extended to Jane.

Having repented of my lack of forgiveness, I am beginning to instead feel genuine sorrow for Jane again. I may even try to reengage with her again, although that likely means facing unfair accusations and anger. Regardless, am I willing to reach out again in an effort to love and forgive her unconditionally? I find it easier to rationalize reasons why I shouldn't, such as her unwillingness to see and be sorry for what she has done.

We appreciate God's mercy when it benefits us but do we appreciate His attributes when they benefit someone who in our view doesn't deserve them? What do you desire for the friend who betrays you, or the boss who fires you, or someone who cheats you, or a close kin who has abused you?

Do you have individuals in your life that are difficult to forgive? Do you find yourself rationalizing your attitude because of their actions—or lack thereof?

_____

_____

_____

_____

What is your role when your offer of apology is rebuffed?

If you feel like your relationship with God is lacking intimacy, spend some time pondering whether there is a person that comes to mind that you are in need of forgiving. Are you holding on to anger as a means of making someone pay or in an attempt to get even with them?

Break free from provocation

Of the few direct statements for parents in the New Testament, two clear warnings are given to not provoke our children:

- *"Fathers, do not provoke your children to anger, but bring them up in the discipline and instruction of the Lord"* (Ephesians 6:4).
- *"Fathers, do not provoke your children, lest they become discouraged"* (Colossians 3:21).

Both times, this exhortation for parents, and fathers specifically, follows the two commands for children to obey their parents. *What's the connection?* Could it be that we have a propensity to provoke our children as a means by which to gain their obedience? Then, rather than gaining sincere obedience, we wind up with raising kids with angry, discouraged hearts. We provoke our kids when we:

- discipline in harsh, punitive ways
- discipline while angry

- regularly find fault
- scold and lecture
- chastise them in front of others
- mock or ridicule them
- hold to standards that we don't apply to ourselves
- fail to admit our mistakes or apologize
- fail to make time to listen and talk with them
- deny them freedom to grow and learn for themselves
- fail to keep promises

On the other hand, some children come to believe that their parents exist to make them happy, and that their demands should take precedence over everything and everyone else. Seated at the helm, they believe they deserve to be the dominant influence and their demands should supersede even those of the parents. They are allowed to interrupt constantly, to demand excessive time and attention from their parents, and to escape the consequences for their irresponsible behaviors. Because they have come to expect their parents to be at their beck and call, when their misguided expectations are not immediately met, they grow angry.

Do either of these two foundational reasons describe how you were raised? What was your internal response as a child? Do you find yourself falling into similar patterns?

_____

_____

_____

_____

Break free from shame

I tend to beat myself up for mistakes long after confessing a wrongdoing and accepting forgiveness. Holding on to self-condemnation disrupts my sleep and makes me feel anxious.

Certainly the cleansing of my heart depends upon my willingness to confess and repent and grieving over my own sin aids this process. (*Blessed are those who mourn!*) However, it is not the mourning over my sin that brings forgiveness. It's God's unconditional forgiveness that does. When I continue to shame myself, the resulting unrest and inner conflict is not caused by how God views me, but by how I view myself.

God's forgiveness is constantly in action. He forgives ALL unrighteousness. There is no sin that can outlast God's forgiveness if we are willing to confess and repent (1 John 1:9). Rather than doubt His forgiveness, after genuine repentance, we need to quit listening to the accuser. Once we are forgiven, our sins are removed from us as far as the east is from the west (Psalm 103:12).

Wouldn't it be wonderful if we could learn to forgive others as Christ forgives us? And wouldn't it be great if we could teach our kids this important principle?

What are the offenses you tend to hold onto? What offenses do you struggle to let go of? Why? Name one way your family can allow forgiveness to flow more readily.

_____

_____

_____

_____

Break free from self-pity

When we choose not to forgive others, it's a sin that causes our hearts to grow bitter and bitterness blinds us to God's grace for others and even for ourselves. In such a state of mind, self-pity easily becomes the narrative.

Self-pity is a crippling emotional mindset that severely distorts ones perception of reality. It creeps into one's thinking easily and subtly and if allowed to linger, takes up residence. Feeling sorry for oneself is not only addictive but also self-perpetuating. Because it feels good to our sin nature, a person, caught up in self-pity, looks for reason not to forgive and most any day offers up plenty of opportunities. "No sin is worse than the sin of self-pity, because it obliterates God and puts self-interest upon the throne," said Oswald Chambers.[9]

Kids need to learn the difference between self-pity and genuine sadness. Sadness is a healthy response to things that are bothersome, but self-pity is not. Self-pity is taking your grief and distorting it so that others owe you something on account of it.

What signs of self-pity do you see in your children? How do you deal with the child who enjoys self-pity?

_____

_____

_____

_____

Break free from unhealthy conflict resolution

Lots of things happen between people that can just be let go of. We tire and get cranky. We say things we don't mean. Kids who are hungry and tired can be completely out of sorts. A large portion of what we let get under our skin is simply a part of living in relationship with others. We just need to be thicker skinned. *"Good sense makes one slow to anger, and it is his glory to overlook an offense"* (Proverbs 19:11).

Some forms of conflict, however, should be addressed. "We never disagree" is not a sign of healthy families. It's how conflicts are managed that determines whether a family's relationships are healthy or not, connected or disconnected, intimate or cold.

Common responses to authentic conflict are often fight-based or flight-based, however. We either blow up or clam up. Neither works. The difficulty with mishandled conflict is that it breaks down communication between two people. We grow angry when we feel attacked and criticized. We grow angry when we feel unheard and uncared for. Then we either attack or withdraw.

Consider the visual on page 76 of "Free to Parent." Do you tend towards flight-based responses such as withdrawing and sulking? Consider what you can do to move towards conflict resolution that leads to forgiveness.

___

___

___

___

To avoid conflict may be cheating someone else out of a chance to be heard. Not being willing to engage in conflict says, "It's your issue—don't tell me about your pain." To engage in conflict does not mean you need to solve another's problem. Nor does it mean you have to agree. Rather, it means you are willing to take the time to try to understand what the other person is feeling. Healthy conflict brings problems to light, gives you a chance to care and empathize, provides an opportunity to break ineffective habits, and restores unity.

Do you find yourself withdrawing to avoid conflict or do you tend towards fight-based responses such as yelling and screaming? What moves you to such responses within your family?

___

___

___

___

Unhealthy ways to handle conflict:
- "Peace at any price" merely buries the issues, which can then fester and explode.
- Suppressing emotions and refusing to engage in communication about certain topics.
- Insults, attacks on character, sarcasm and disgust lead to either heightened frustration or withdrawal. *"But if you bite and devour one other, watch out that you are not consumed by one another"* (Galatians 5:15).
- Refusing to accept another's attempts to apologize.

Principles for wise management of conflict:
- Go to prayer first. Examine your own heart first and ask God for wisdom and discernment before speaking and acting.
- Make your goal that of understanding each other and not necessarily agreeing.
- Recognize emotions as signposts and look for the message behind the words.
- Purpose to empathize. Put yourself figuratively in the other person's place. This helps prevent defensiveness because we acknowledge what the other person is feeling. To empathize is to be compassionate. *"Put on then, as God's chosen ones, holy and beloved, compassionate hearts, kindness, humility, meekness, and patience, bearing with one another and, if one has a complaint against another, forgiving each other; as the Lord has forgiven you, so you also must forgive"* (Colossians 3:12-13).
- Treat your family members in valuable ways. Let them know that even in the midst of conflict, you value them and love them so that they will feel safe to share what they are really feeling.
- Ask thoughtful questions which helps uncover the concerns of the other person and takes the focus off the disagreement.
- Be good at repenting, by readily admitting your own mistakes and apologizing for them.

GROUP STUDY SECTION

The Beatitudes: Cultivating a merciful, forgiving mindset

My granddaughter Kate was angry.

Her little brother Will had come into her room (again) and taken out her American Girl dolls (again) and lost her favorite American Girl ice skate. Obviously, a very precarious situation. My daughter Erin dealt with it (again) and made Will help her search the room all to no avail. The ice skate was gone.

Erin looked up at Will and said, "Will, you lost Kate's toy. You are going to have to apologize and ask for forgiveness."

"Ka—ate. I'm sorry. I didn't mean to lose the ice skate." Will's voice trembled as he talked.

But Kate didn't respond. Instead she hauled across the room and tackled him. (I'm learning this is what happens when you grow up sandwiched between two wild brothers!)

Erin was shocked! Will was apologizing and he was just a toddler...why would a seven-year-old tackle him?

Because she was struggling to forgive. Her anger over the situation overwhelmed her emotions (and clearly her self-control) and she just lost it.

Erin and Kate had a long talk about mercy and forgiveness and how three-year-old brothers may be obnoxious but they are also precious children of God. Kate apologized and they worked out strategies to learn to forgive and show mercy.

To me, this story was a good reminder of human nature: We are all sinners. We each struggle with mercy and forgiveness. And there are times that many of us probably want to haul off and tackle a person who has offended us.

The key to cultivating a merciful, forgiving mindset is not teaching kids not to have natural emotions like anger, but how to deal with them the right way. It's a process, but its one that will change your kids.

The Fifth Beatitude: Forgiving Others

*"Blessed are the merciful,
for they shall receive mercy."*
Matthew 5:7

Because of the terrible way King David sinned, some wonder why God showed such great mercy to him. Perhaps it's because the one who forgives gains forgiveness. David showed unfailing mercy to Saul on several occasions even though Saul's aim was to kill David.

As one God has been merciful to, we should offer this mercy to others; to those who are weaker, who weep and mourn, and even to those who have wronged us.

Discussion questions

1. Do you find forgiveness easy or difficult? Who is it hardest for you to forgive?

2. What about your kids? Does forgiveness come easily to them or do they struggle?

3. What types of offenses make your kids most angry? What about you?

4. Have you ever been shown mercy after an offense? How did it make you feel?

5. How are you teaching your kids about God's mercy?

I pray that mercy and grace will be the flavor of your homes and that anger will be driven out. May forgiveness flow in all directions and may God's will be done within your family. Here is the scripture passage for this session to meditate on:

Matthew 18:21-35
The Parable of the Unforgiving Servant

21 Then Peter came up and said to him, "Lord, how often will my brother sin against me, and I forgive him? As many as seven times?" 22 Jesus said to him, "I do not say to you seven times, but seventy-seven times.

23 "Therefore the kingdom of heaven may be compared to a king who wished to settle accounts with his servants. 24 When he began to settle, one was brought to him who owed him ten thousand talents. 25 And since he could not pay, his master ordered him to be sold, with his wife and children and all that he had, and payment to be made. 26 So the servant fell on his knees, imploring him, 'Have patience with me, and I will pay you everything.' 27 And out of pity for him, the master of that servant released him and forgave him the debt. 28 But when that same servant went out, he found one of his fellow servants who owed him a hundred denarii, and seizing him, he began to choke him, saying, 'Pay what you owe.' 29 So his fellow servant fell down and pleaded with him, 'Have patience with me, and I will pay you.' 30 He refused and went and put him in prison until he should pay the debt. 31 When his fellow servants saw what had taken place, they were greatly distressed, and they went and reported to their master all that had taken place. 32 Then his master summoned him and said to him, 'You wicked servant! I forgave you all that debt because you pleaded with me. 33 And should not you have had mercy on your fellow servant, as I had mercy on you?' 34 And in anger his master delivered him to the jailers, until he should pay all his debt. 35 So also my heavenly Father will do to every one of you, if you do not forgive your brother from your heart."

Session 8

REPLACE GRUMBLING WITH GRATITUDE

Start this session by reading chapter 8 in *Free to Parent*.

My husband and I spent ten wonderful days in Hawaii this past summer. We spent the evenings and nights on a cruise ship and the days exploring what each beautiful island had to offer. It was certainly a dream vacation! Yet on last day, when we discovered that our return trip was cancelled and we were rerouted on a longer, later flight, I gave myself permission to grumble. After all, we now getting home nine hours later, missing a Father's Day gathering with our family, and we were flying from Honolulu to Seattle to Atlanta before arriving home in Austin. I was tired. And mad. And I felt justified in letting the spokesperson know it. I felt entitled to at least a better seat or extra miles. Something for this misery.

The more I grumbled internally the more miserable I grew, however. Midway through the second leg of the journey, I grew convicted of the silliness of my attitude. The original flight had been cancelled for safety reasons. Something I should be grateful for. And they were getting us home on the same day as planned by flying us through two airports across the country from each other before landing us in Austin. No one was dismissive—they were simply doing their best with a difficult situation. No one responded to my complaining with rudeness. In fact, we were treated kindly and respectfully at all points. As I chose to let go of grumbling, I was actually able to be content and enjoy the extra time to read, to watch a movie, and to put a smile on my face when we finally landed in Austin.

Sometimes a tiny attitude shift is all it takes to bring new perspective. And by teaching our kids to be slow to grumble and quick to find joy, we can help them to see Christ's mercy in every situation.

Replacing grumbling with gratitude: Parenting kids towards contentment

The giving of thanks is not an option but a directive. *"And whatever you do, in word or deed, do everything in the name of the Lord Jesus, giving thanks to God the Father through Him"* (Colossians 3:17). When facing troublesome circumstances, I remind myself of the apostle Paul's words in 1 Thessalonians 5:16-18 *"Rejoice always, pray without ceasing, give thanks in all circumstances for this is the will of God in Christ Jesus for you."* This reminder serves to keep the mud from blinding my vision in those troubling times when I am feeling overwhelmed and frustrated.

The giving of thanks is always uplifting. What an amazing privilege and opportunity we have to *"enter his gates with thanksgiving and into His courts with praise!"* (Psalm 100:4a). It's where prayers are answered and miracles occur. It is where we find contentment and peace. It is where our worries and anxieties are defeated. It's where we get past ourselves.

It's simple yet powerful, uncomplicated yet amazingly liberating. But it's very easy to overlook. Gratitude is healing:
- When you are tired, gratitude will refresh you.
- When you are worried, gratitude will calm you.

- When you are irritable, gratitude will sooth your frayed nerves.
- When you are angry, gratitude will move you to forgive.
- When you need guidance, gratitude will lift your eyes toward Him.
- When you feel discouraged, gratitude will resurrect hope.
- When you feel stressed and overwhelmed, gratitude will lighten your burden.

Much research, in both secular and faith circles, has been done on the health benefits of gratitude. According to an article posted in the Huffington Post, being grateful makes for better friendships, boosts morale, helps sleep come easier, benefits the heart and immune system, and is even linked to better grades.[10] Elizabeth Huebeck, in an article posted on WebMD, had this to say about gratitude:

> Can just a positive emotion such as gratitude guarantee better health? It may be a dramatic departure from what we've been taught about how to get healthier, but the connection between gratitude and health actually goes back a long way. 'Thousands of years of literature talk about the benefits of cultivating gratefulness as a virtue," says University of California Davis psychology professor Robert Emmons. Throughout history, philosophers and religious leaders have extolled gratitude as a virtue integral to health and well-being. Grateful people—those who perceive gratitude as a permanent trait rather than a temporary state of mind—have an edge on the not-so-grateful when it comes to health, according to Emmon's research on gratitude.[11]

What are you grateful for today? Can you name anything about your current struggles that you could be grateful for?

_____

_____

_____

_____

Break free from complaining

My husband and I went to Israel a few years ago. (If you think you are sensing a theme here, you are! My husband and I have loved to travel in our "older years.") A highlight of the trip was walking through the wilderness regions where the Israelites roamed for forty years. I now understand why they had such a propensity to whine and complain. I think I would have been right there with them! This dusty, barren terrain, outside the Promise Land, would not have been my idea of where to hang out. Yet Paul indicated, in 1 Corinthians 10:10, that their complaining opened the door to destruction by our destroyer.

We often give ourselves permission to have an ungrateful attitude when things don't seem to be going our way. But instead of making things better, this only opens the door to destructive thinking and acting. We must shake free from these attitudes and allow gratitude to transform our thinking instead, regardless of what we face in life. *"Do <u>all things</u> without grumbling or disputing; so that you will may be blameless and innocent, children of God without blemish in the midst of a crooked and twisted generation, among whom you shine as lights in the world"* (Philippians 2:14-15, emphasis added).

When I am not abiding in a mindset of gratitude, I quickly begin to grumble and complain and focus on what I don't like. Grumbling is contagious, but so is the giving of thanks! And one drives the other out.

Ponder this: Do you complain because of trouble or do you heap trouble on yourself because you complain? Does a foul mood cause you to grumble or does grumbling cause a foul mood?

_____
_____
_____
_____

Think of a time when grumbling served to dampen your perspective.

_____
_____
_____
_____

What about your children? Do you hear them express your own negative opinions?

_____
_____
_____
_____

Here is some advice to mothers written back in 1878 in **Don'ts for Mothers**:

> Don't talk over troubles around the child. Few things can be more harmful to the health than to see dismal countenances and to hear constant lamentations.
> Don't allow the child to whine and fret, as there is nothing worse for the health. Habits of discontent develop chronic dis-

eases and a peevish child has little chance of growing up healthy or happy.[12]

It's one thing to share difficulties, and to seek prayer and counsel on behalf of our children. It's quite another thing to complain and grumble about them. Gratitude is our defense against becoming overwhelmed and hopeless as parents. We don't have to wait for our spouse or kids to change in order to be grateful. Our kids need to see—and hear—parents who believe what God says, parents whose hearts are at peace and not overwhelmed by the circumstances of life, nor by their children!

Break free from covetousness

I love being around people. And I love to enjoy the many personalities that God put on earth. But, there are times that I notice myself falling into an ungrateful mindset doing so. I find myself thinking things like *wouldn't it be nice to have those gorgeous boots for winter?* or *what a fun car that would be to drive!*

I dare say that wishing for more than one possesses—or covetousness—is a problem for many Americans. And it doesn't stop with looks or possessions. We also desire to be other than who God has created us to be. "If only I could sing/draw/write/speak/run like her." And we pass along a desire for more to our children because we don't want to see them lack for anything either. Jesus said this about covetousness in Luke 12:15, *"Take care and be on your guard against all covetousness, for one's life does not consist in the abundance of his possessions."*

As U.S. citizens, we are among the most privileged in the world, but we can become so entrenched in our richness that we can fail to see how blessed we are. Instead we focus on what we don't possess as a standard for what to strive for. It's an easy habit to develop to compare ourselves negatively to others, or to regard our possessions against what we don't have. *If only I had more money, more connections, a nicer husband, more obedient children, better looks, nicer clothes, the latest iPhone, a better job.*

What if we were instead to consider how fortunate we are in comparison to so many others? When I feel sad over the minor limitations of having an artificial hip, I need only to think of those who can never avail themselves of such medical advances. When I whine about our broken health care system, I need only to consider families living in the Ebola stricken regions of western Africa. When I begin to see my home as inadequate, I need only to turn my thoughts towards those living perpetually without a roof over their heads, or to martyrs for our faith who abide in tiny prison cells. When I covet those sitting in first class airplane seating, on the way back to the cramped economy seating, I need only to consider the millions around the world who will never even set foot inside an airplane.

To be content with what I have, taking my eyes off what I lack, is a wise aim. And it's freeing. *"Keep your life free from love of money, and be content with what you have, for He has said, 'I will never leave you nor forsake you' "* (Hebrews 13:5).

What do you find yourself coveting and how do you see your kids mimicking you?

_____

_____

_____

_____

It's easy at times to even feel discontent with our children, wishing they were somehow different than they are. But God chose you to train your specific kids for a season. And He designed them just as they are, with an intentional set of strengths and weaknesses, for a unique purpose. Along with their strengths, we can be grateful for their weaknesses, which God will use to drive them to Him. Love the kids you have. No part of them is a mistake.

In which ways do you find yourself growing discontent with the kids God has blessed you with?

_____
_____
_____
_____

Break free from fretfulness

I often fret when I don't know what to do. I'll fear making a wrong decision and instead of prayerfully walking forward, I allow myself to live in angst. This happens especially when the choice is in regards to important matters such as employment or discipline or school choice. Not having clear direction is troubling, but relying on our own musings, and over-thinking each side of a decision, often leads to even more confusion and angst. There is an answer to this fretfulness: *"If any of you lacks wisdom, let him ask God, who gives generously to all without reproach, and it will be given to him. But let him ask in faith, with no doubting, for the one who doubts is like a wave of the sea that is driven and tossed by the wind. For that person must not suppose that he will receive anything from the Lord; he is a double-minded man, unstable in all his ways"* (James 1:5-8).

Ponder these verses in James and consider how much of the confusion you feel is a result of a fretful mindset. Does fretting clarify a decision or make it more difficult to act?

_____
_____
_____
_____

What a promise we have in Matthew 21:22: *"And whatever you ask in prayer, you will receive, if you have faith."* The moment I turn my eyes toward Jesus, thanking Him for wisdom in the situation I face, peace takes over. While answers don't always come immediately, I begin to see things in a different light and peace replaces my fretting. By the time a decision needs to be made, the answer comes, often in an unexpected way. But it does come. He always provides light enough to see to the next corner and by the time I get there, I know which way I need to turn. Right in those dark, confusing times, as I choose to thank and trust Him, He responds to my offering of gratitude with hopeful assurance. He is our loving, faithful, all-knowing Father who desires that we turn to Him with our needs.

Group Study Section

The Beatitudes: Cultivating a content heart

Not long ago, I grew sullen about a pending trip to Oregon. I go on a monthly basis to help take care of my aging mom, and while I consider it a great privilege to care for her, it can also be trying. And, after an exhausting few weeks at school, the last thing I wanted to do was spend another week in Oregon at my mom's nursing home. I allowed myself to grumble inwardly about it.

Not only was I leaving again for five days, but also plans to take my mom to visit family had fallen through. That meant I alone would be there to keep her content and happy. I would be the only one around to listen to her same stories, answer her same questions and calm her familiar anxieties. Spending extended time with an Alzheimer's patient can be exhausting and I gave myself permission to complain silently about it. Soon my mood grew negative. Then I complained to Glen. And to Erin. As I began to feel sorry for myself, it dawned on me that grumbling had actually caused my mood to spiral downward and not the other way around. So I began to think instead about the privilege I am granted to be able to see my mom each month; that my place of employment allows it; that Glen stands behind me; that my family understands; and that I am healthy enough to travel and spend time with my mother in this declining season of her life.

As I began to reflect on my trip with these thoughts in mind, my mood lifted and the trip took on a wholly different perspective. In hindsight, this trip turned out to be a particularly gratifying experience.

A grateful heart may be one of the truest signs of a surrendered heart and one that is impossible to teach unless we first embrace it ourselves.

> ### The Sixth Beatitude: An Undivided Heart
>
> *"Blessed are the pure in heart,*
> *for they shall see God."*
> Matthew 5:8
>
> People who are pure in heart are grateful people. To be pure in heart refers to an inner moral purity, an undivided heart that is devoted to God in motivation, in thought, and in action. Those who express a consistently grateful spirit are individuals who enjoy a deep intimacy with God. Grumbling, covetousness, or other deceptions do not blind them. Instead, they view life through the lens of faith. A constant state of gratitude reflects an undivided heart!

Discussion questions

1. Think of a pessimistic outlook that you currently hold onto. How can you reframe it to consider the good that can come out of the challenges you face?

2. In which ways can dealing with those difficult people in your life be seen as beneficial?

3. Think back on a difficult situation or challenge that you have faced. How in hindsight has this experience strengthened you and made you into a better person?

4. Being generous with your time and treasure is one way to foster gratitude because the act of being generous puts the focus on others. Think of ways your family can practice generosity.

I pray that the fragrance of gratitude will define your homes and that your children will be content with what they have and who they are in Christ. Here is the scripture passage for this session to meditate on:

Psalm 100:1-5

¹ Make a joyful noise to the LORD, all the earth!
² Serve the LORD with gladness!
Come into his presence with singing!
³ Know that the LORD, he is God!
It is he who made us, and we are his;
we are his people, and the sheep of his pasture.
⁴ Enter his gates with thanksgiving,
and his courts with praise!
Give thanks to him; bless his name!
⁵ For the LORD is good;
his steadfast love endures forever,
and his faithfulness to all generations.

Session 9

REPLACE DISTRACTEDNESS WITH REST

Begin this session by reading chapter 9 in *Free to Parent*.

I spoke to our grammar school students at school about Psalms 46 last year. When I came to the verse *"Be still and know that I am God,"* I looked out into the audience and considered the sweet faces gazing back at me. I realized that I was speaking to boys and girls who definitely knew what it meant to *hold still*, but I wondered whether they comprehended, or even knew how to *be still*.

Today's kids live a fast-paced life. They carry complex gadgets that can connect them with anything or anyone whenever they wish. They fill their minds with a constant stream of disruption. They always have somewhere to go, something to do and something to entertain them. As a result, they often fail to gain vital spiritual disciplines. And they rarely learn to *be still*.

My kids were in high school when cell phones were first introduced. I remember saying to a friend emphatically, "I will never buy one." (I really believed that!) She wholehearted agreed that she wouldn't either. We did not see the need, nor did we want to grow dependent on such a machine.

Fast forward twenty years and I have (clearly) changed my tune. And in many ways, that's a good thing. I am dependent on my iPhone for many things and consider it a necessity in order to stay in contact especially with those I hold most dear. I love my cell phone and am in no way considering going without it. But there is something I long for from those pre-cell phone years that I desire to bring back. Rather than immediately reaching for my iPhone when I have a concern for someone, I want to restore the practice of going on my knees instead. I want to live out a faith that turns to God first—to be connected foremost to Him. I want to make prayer a vibrant habit in my life and learn to better resist my cell phone.

I recognize how it can distract me, make me restless, and replace prayer. As an adult, I comprehend these problems; but what about our children who are still maturing? Raising kids in a wired world has benefits to be sure, but as they are learning to properly use these tools, they need wise boundaries that are vigilantly upheld. Otherwise, they can easily become accustomed to a continual state of mental restlessness and unaware of anything different.

The digital world is not the only source of distraction is our lives, however. It merely offers an easy path for a heart and mind *already prone* to distraction. Before I owned any digital gadgets, I found all sorts of internal ways to be distracted from seeking God: trying to please others, over thinking issues, worrying about my kids. It wasn't until I developed practices that kept me in-tune with His voice, that I learned to live a peace-filled life, free from the fears that threatened to engulf me.

Replacing distractedness with rest: Parenting our kids so that they gain vital disciplines of the heart and mind

Learning to *be still* is an essential discipline. It's about keeping the mind focused on what one should be attending to, which, in case you missed it, is God. Kids need daily practice so they can be meditative and prayerful so they can grow in this habit. By intentionally giving our kids the time to be still with God, we nurture the development of vital disciplines of the heart and mind.

How comfortable are you with stillness or do you immediately go looking for some noise to fill the space? How about your kids?

_____

_____

_____

_____

What internal patterns do you hold on to that distract you from seeking God?

_____

_____

_____

_____

Break free from overusing technology

Adults and kids alike benefit by setting clear guidelines for technology and by regularly disconnecting from it. We need *tech-free time alone* in order to make room for vital disciplines of the heart and mind to grow. We also need to establish *tech-free zones* in order to connect with family members, such as meal times, car rides, and date nights with our spouse or kids. These are precious times when important discussions occur and connection is developed.

What steps are you taking to ensure times in your life, and in your kids, that are free from the distractions of your screen gadgets? Take time this week to establish important boundaries and then make a plan to stick to them. You may be surprised at the time you gain back with your family, as well as the positive impact this has on your relationships.

_____

_____

_____

_____

Break free from anxiousness

Peace is one of the most amazing gifts from God we can embrace. *"Do not be anxious about anything, but in everything by prayer and supplication with thanksgiving let your requests be made known to God. And the peace of God, which surpasses all understanding, will guard your hearts and minds in Christ Jesus"* (Philippians 4:6-7). For years, this verse has been my refrain when anxiety threatens to engulf my mind. How amazing that we can even have peace even when we are experiencing stormy times.

In Psalm 46:1-2a it says that *"God is our refuge and strength, a very present help in trouble. Therefore, we will not fear though the earth give way."* This inner state of being becomes a part of who we are not by default but by intentional, spiritual practices. To be still in the midst of fear and anxiety seems improbable, yet it's exactly what we are told to do—to turn our hearts and minds to an *ever-present* God, our refuge and our strength. We need to be still at those times of challenge when we are most prone to fretting and taking matters into our own hands. We need to be still throughout each day so that we can hear God, who speaks to us continuously, offering us wisdom and counsel.

When you have a few free moments, are you more likely to turn to your phone or to be still and converse with God?

_____
_____
_____
_____

Who do you turn to first when you find yourself in the midst of a storm? How can you retrain your mind to turn to Christ first?

_____
_____
_____
_____

Break free from an inconsistent prayer life

Are you easily distracted from prayer? Do your find your thoughts turning to other things the moment you purpose to pray? I am deeply convicted that the greatest work we are called to do is to pray, yet I can often answer yes to both of those questions.

The truth is that we all have *as much time to pray as we need*. We simply don't allow ourselves. A mind used to distraction simply does not want to focus badly enough. Prayer is a spiritual discipline that takes deep determination and intentional effort. Distraction is the default.

Joey, my nine-year-old grandson, will at times stubbornly refuse to admit his mistakes. The more he is pushed to concede, the tighter he holds onto a defiant mindset. I have begun to pray at those difficult moments with Joey. And he has yet to refuse my offers to pray with him. I am careful not to use prayer as an opportunity to lecture however. Instead, I speak affirming words that define who he is becoming in the Lord and the character he is working towards. Prayer softens Joey's heart and melts his resolve to be defiant. It centers him and draws him back in.

We will never be a perfect parent but we can always be parents who pray, which is really our most effective way to shape their lives and influence their futures. If we would decide to give ourselves consistently up to prayer, and be diligent in this quest, how different would our lives be? *"Let us also lay aside every weight, and sin which clings so closely, and let us run with endurance the race that is set before us"* (Hebrews 12:1b).

What are the weights you need to lay aside that get in the way of prayer?

_____

_____

_____

_____

Do you have specific time set aside every day for prayer? If not, write down some times right now that you will set aside for prayer.

_____

_____

_____

_____

Break free from shallow thinking

Kate, my seven-year-old granddaughter, loves to create poetry and songs. She has filled a thick journal with them. This past year, as she memorized long chunks of scripture and learned hymns in her music class at school, her creations began to be filled with spiritual aspirations. While they can be amusing, coming from a young girl, they come from a mind that is filling with thoughts about God. Here's a cute example of a recent song she wrote:

Heavenly God, spread your Joy!
Oh God, you love me! You love us! You love all!
Oh good God, you love us all.
And you help us not to get sick because no one likes being sick.
But we love you, heavenly God!
Bless the Lord!

We are bombarded with so much information but how much of it actually fosters the growth of wisdom and virtue? And what is filling the memory banks of your children? Many erroneously believe that growing memory skills is not important anymore. With information available at our fingertips, why go through the tedious task of memorizing things we can simply look up? Yet, it is in the memorizing of scripture that something profound happens within one's heart.

I find myself thinking on scripture in a new and deeper way once I commit it to memory. Verses that I have stored in my heart come readily to mind during the day. Like any other discipline, memorization gets easier with practice. I am a better memorizer today than I was in earlier years because I now make it a practice to be so. *"Your words were found, and I ate them, and your words became to me a joy and the delight of my heart, for I am called by your name, O LORD, God of hosts"* (Jeremiah 15:16).

How has technology impacted your personal practices of memorizing?

_____

_____

_____

_____

What Bible verses or passages do you want to memorize in the coming months?

Group study section

The Beatitudes: Cultivating a peaceful mind

What is God like?

How will He act towards us?

Such questions resonate deeply in the human spirit, and the answers affect not only our daily experiences, but also our character and our vision for life itself. Seeking after God, in all His fullness, is the only path to a peace-filled life. He is the God of peace! But how do we teach our kids about an incomprehensible God? If we could grasp Him, He would be like us, but He is beyond us. Yet in times of stillness, the Spirit of God reveals the things of God to our soul in a deeply tender way:

> *"For who knows a person's thoughts except the spirit of that person, which is in him? So also no one comprehends the thoughts of God except the Spirit of God. Now we have received not the spirit of the world, but the Spirit who is from God, that we might understand the things freely given us by God. And we impart this in words not taught by human wisdom but taught by the Spirit, interpreting spiritual truths to those who are spiritual. The natural person does not accept the things of the Spirit of God, for they are folly to him, and he is not able to understand them because they are spiritually discerned"* (1 Corinthians 2:11-14).

We tend towards thinking like a natural person and we prefer to ignore or even reject what we cannot understand. Only in humble faith and in wonder are we able to grasp God to any measure, but this requires an undistracted, peaceful mind, one that can contemplate and meditate on the things of God and one that is attune to His voice. It is in our inattention and in our shadow processing that we cease to wonder about God: *"And He is before all things, and in Him all things hold together"* (Colossians 1:17).

> ## The Seventh Beatitude: Peace Within
>
> *"Blessed are the peacemakers,*
> *for they shall be called the sons of God."*
> **Matthew 5:9**
>
> Those who sow peace are able to do so because they have overcome evil within their own hearts and are at peace within. This only comes when we have settled within our souls whom we abide in and whom we listen to. Those who are listening to the voice of the Lord will not be deafened by the opinions and arguments of others. In a world filled with noises all demanding attention, do you still hear Him?

Discussion questions

1. Are you more prone towards thinking about how God can make things better for you or on who He is? Are your goals about the betterment of life or on growing closer to God?

2. What issues in life serve to make you anxious and distraught? What practices can you develop to bring peace to your heart in the midst of these issues?

3. In which ways do you plan to reduce distraction in your life and in the lives of your children?

4. When are you able to experience a mind at rest, one that hears God daily? How can you build in more times to do so?

I pray that the God of peace invades your hearts and homes and that He becomes more real to you each and everyday. I pray that your children gain the spiritual disciplines vital to a life of prayer and ability to rest in Him. Here is the scripture passage for this session to meditate on:

Proverbs 2:1-5

¹ My son, if you receive my words and treasure up my commandments with you, ² making your ear attentive to wisdom, and inclining your heart to understanding; ³ yes, if you call out for insight and raise your voice for understanding, ⁴ if you seek it like silver and search for it as for hidden treasures, ⁵ then you will understand the fear of the Lord and find the knowledge of God.

Session 10

REPLACE HOPELESSNESS WITH HOPE

Begin this session by reading chapter 10 in *Free to Parent*.

Kara is 16. She is a lovely young woman who desires to do well and please God. But often she finds herself feeling sad for no reason at all. When she feels this way, she cries herself to sleep, avoids her friends and has a hard time concentrating at school. Her greatest fear is that someday she won't be able to climb out of these depressive episodes and that her life will therefore be ruined.

It's not that she is doing anything rebellious during these times, simply that she gives up. Doing well in school, pleasing her parents and teachers, and honoring God, all feel out of reach and unbearably overwhelming. So she quits. Then she beats herself up for giving up and slides further into hopelessness!

Lately however, with some help from a counselor, Kara has begun to grow awareness for the depression that plagues her. And with the help of her family, friends, and a trained doctor, she has been able to slowly work her way out of the haze of depression and into a feeling of hope .

I've met with Kara for years and am so proud of the progress she has made. The last time we met, she asked me to tell her sweet mom to "love her less." To clarify what she meant, she explained with a grin on her face that, "while I want her to understand me during difficult times, I also really need her to hold me accountable to standards and not agree with my excuses." As I sat there looking somewhat perplexed, she went on to say "when she sympathizes with the excuses I cough up, it give me permission to embrace them even though I don't really want to. But then I have an easy exit off a challenging path I should remain on, and wind up sitting on the sideline feeling sorry for myself."

I left this meeting feeling so proud and full of hope for this wise young lady who is figuring out how to walk in God's promises for her. She, like most other students I know, deeply desires to see her life have meaning and purpose. She doesn't want to give up on her hopes and dreams, although the words coming out of her mouth can sometimes indicate the opposite. While she certainly needs grace at times, she also needs goals and standards that are not unnecessarily lowered during difficult stretches. Kara fears failure. She struggles with depression. But lowering the bar does not mitigate this fear or help her to overcome her issues. Rather it removes all chances of success in her eyes, which she fears even more.

At times, do you find yourself inclined to embrace excuses for your children and lower expectations in an attempt to make them feel hopeful about themselves?

_____

_____

_____

_____

Replacing hopelessness with hope: Parenting our kids with our hope placed firmly in God

God breathes spiritual aspirations into each of His children. With your own kids, you may find them hidden at times, buried beneath attempts to hide their shortcomings. Sooner or later, however, they will discover (first with dismay but then actually with relief) that they are not sufficient in and of themselves to walk in God's calling for them; rather they were created for Jesus to reign in their hearts and accomplish His work in and through them.

Through her struggles and failings, Kara is growing keenly aware of her need for Him. With loving support and guidance that encourages her to keep her eyes on Jesus, she will get to the other side of this battle and walk in her God-given aspirations. I am grateful that her parents understand this and expect her to keep climbing. And that Kara herself is willing to hope for herself and her future.

There is a silver lining even in the darkest seasons when your children feel despondent and their self-concept is utterly deflated. How can you spur true hope for them during these difficult stretches as they mature and grow towards spiritual maturity?

_____

_____

_____

_____

How we envision God determines both the direction and the quality of our lives. That's why it's so important to get it right; a low view of God destroys the gospel. The greatest service we can do for the next generation is to teach them to place their hope in Jesus who is our only *sure and steadfast anchor of the soul* (Hebrews 6:19). Our greatest role as parents is to guide our children to *"attain to the unity of the faith and of the knowledge of the Son of God, to mature* manhood, to the measure of the stature of the fullness of Christ, so that [they] may no longer be children, tossed to and fro by the waves and carried about by every wind of doctrine, by human cunning, by craftiness in deceitful schemes"* (Ephesians 4:13-14).

What do you find yourself placing false hope in?

Attempting to find hope in *anything but Christ* results in fear and despair, but as believers we need not fear because God has *put His seal on us and given us His Spirit in our hearts as a guarantee* (2 Corinthians 1:22). He not only reigns over all the earth but He will also reign in a yielded heart. He promises to be our strength and upholds us with His righteous right hand (Isaiah 41:10) when we place our dreams and plans wholly in His hands. I am so very grateful that God not only saves our souls but He also saves us from despair, from disappointment, from regret, and from hopelessness.

Break free from discouragement

I firmly believe that God imparts vision to parents for each of their children: vision that aligns their unique temperaments and gifting with His calling. While it's deceptive (even discouraging) to tell your kids that they can become anything they want to be, they will find lasting hope in knowing they can become *anything God wants them to be*. Not only do they find hope, but they discover true freedom as well.

It's easy to lose hope however when things don't turn out as we expect: when your child fails or makes a big mistake, or faces a seemingly insurmountable obstacle, or slides into a dark hole, or is hurt and rejected by others. It's easy, when hope has diminished, to resort back to approaches that disconnect us from our children at the very times they need our connection and support the most.

Hold on patiently and persistently to that vision God has laid in your heart for your kids, however, because God works in every heart to bring conformation to His will. He is nearer than you think and will do more than you expect. You won't necessarily see what God is doing in your children but He makes no idle stroke. What we picture in our minds and the work God is doing within our children is often entirely different. We may not always see evidence but we can patiently hope for what we do not see (Romans 8:24-25). Let go of fear and hold on to vision. He will accomplish His purposes in both you and your children.

Break free to be the parent God called you to be

Consider the chapters of *Free to Parent*. Is there one that spoke to you more personally than another? Are there changes in perspective you feel lead to make regarding your role as a parent? Consider something you feel impressed to implement or change from each chapter and how it can change your parenting and help you feel free to parent in the way God called you to.

Replace you with him: We are equipped and empowered by Jesus. We are qualified by His work in us and not by what we do ourselves. *In which ways do you need to get out of the way so that your children learn reliance on God and not on you?*

_____

_____

_____

_____

Replace obedience with desire: It's the spirit of God that leads us to obedience. It's not our standards or rules, which are necessary for guidance and direction, but have little power to motivate and change the heart. *What are you doing to allow for a genuine desire for obedience to grow in your child's heart?*

Replace discipline with discipleship: Discipleship hinges upon what you model by your life. It's about you following Jesus and your kids following you. *What practices in your own life need to improve as you disciple your kids?*

Replace control with connection: Control breeds fear. Connection breeds safety. *In which ways can you let go of unnecessary control and nurture connection instead?*

Replace complacency with growth: Are your kids gaining intellectual, emotional, and spiritual muscle of their own or do they prefer to rely on others to do the "heavy lifting" for them? *In what practical ways can you motivate your children to grow rather than allow them to become complacent?*

_____
_____
_____
_____

Replace lectures with love: Kids tune out nagging and lectures. They crave connection, however, especially when they feel ashamed over wrongdoing. *At those times when you need to address misbehavior and hold to firm expectations, how can you also weave in loving acceptance?*

_____
_____
_____
_____

Replace anger with forgiveness: Jesus was betrayed for no particular reason, yet He freely forgave. Likewise, we must not let anger and bitterness prevent us from walking in forgiveness. *Is there a family member, a friend, a co-worker, or anyone that you are holding onto a right to be angry with? Spend some time considering a pathway that leads not only to forgiveness but also to resolution, if possible.*

_____
_____
_____
_____

Replace grumbling with gratitude: Is the lens by which you view life and others tainted more by grumbling or by gratitude? *Write down what moves you to grumble and purpose to be grateful (even if it is in some small way) instead.*

Replace distractedness with rest: We are not designed to experience life in a state of anxious striving. *What distracts you from seeking a daily resting place in Christ? What are you doing about it?*

Replace hopelessness with hope: *What makes you feel hopeless at times? What do you worry most about regarding your children? Write down 2-3 verses that give you hope and serve to make Jesus "the sure and steadfast of your soul"? Then memorize these verses so that they are hidden in your heart.*

Group Study Section

The Beatitudes: Cultivating freedom to parent as He calls you to

When Erin was a baby, I listened intently to parenting experts in the Christian field, and I diligently tried to apply all that I learned. I was determined to make Erin obey. I tried to control her behavior and punished her for wrongdoing, but instead of the incredible joy and hope I felt when I first held her in my arms, I found myself distressed over her behavior and fearful over her future. But slowly, it dawned on me that by trying to perfectly follow prescribed rule-driven strategies, I was missing the mark somehow. I was off course, trapped on a dead-end road and I was leading her off course as well.

I began to gain freedom, however, when I learned to rely first and foremost on guidance and direction that God whispered specifically to me for each of my children. I began to take on a different parenting mindset, which over the years has resulted in writing *Free to Parent*. What delights and amazes me the most is that it wound up being a joint project with my lovely daughter, Erin.

> **The Eighth Beatitude: Standing Firmly and Freely in the Truth**
>
> *"Blessed are those who are persecuted for righteousness sake,*
> *for theirs is the kingdom of Heaven.*
> **Matthew 5:10**
>
> While we do not experience the type of persecution many believers around the world face, Jesus brings insults and malice into the realm of persecution, which can be very prevalent in Christian circles, especially as it relates to how we parent our children.
>
> When judgment, gossip, slander, jealousy, and self-serving indignation permeate the parent culture in Christian churches and schools, the environment takes on a fragrance of divisiveness. Many wind up experiencing deep hurt and rejection and no pain feels greater than those we experience on behalf of our children. Jesus said, *"For with the judgment you pronounce you will be judged, and with the measure you use it will be measured to you"* (Matthew 7:2). We should worry less about what others think and grow free in Christ to parent our kids as His spirit leads each of us. Rather than judging and rebuking each other, we should instead link arms together in prayer and encouragement, united by our love in Christ.

Discussion questions

1. Do you at times feel judged for how you parent? What are you judged for?

2. Do you find yourself measuring other parents by how their kids behave?

3. Who or what determines how you choose to discipline your kids?

4. Consider how we are to treat each other as brothers and sisters in the Lord? In which ways should our treatment of children be the same? Different?

I pray that God will teach you to gently lead your young, to seek Him first on their behalf, to love and cherish your children as He does, and to trust them into His Hands as the one who will accomplish the deeper work of changing their hearts. May you find peace in Him. Here is the scripture passage for this session to meditate on:

Colossians 3:12-17

[12] Put on then, as God's chosen ones, holy and beloved, compassionate hearts, kindness, humility, meekness, and patience, [13] bearing with one another and, if one has a complaint against another, forgiving each other; as the Lord has forgiven you, so you also must forgive. [14] And above all these put on love, which binds everything together in perfect harmony. [15] And let the peace of Christ rule in your hearts, to which indeed you were called in one body. And be thankful. [16] Let the word of Christ dwell in you richly, teaching and admonishing one another in all wisdom, singing psalms and hymns and spiritual songs, with thankfulness in your hearts to God. [17] And whatever you do, in word or deed, do everything in the name of the Lord Jesus, giving thanks to God the Father through him.

Endnotes

[1] *Dictionary.com*, www.dictionary.reference.com/browse/self-esteem (accessed 26 July 2015)
[2] Oswald Chambers, *My Utmost for His Highest* (Discovery House Publisher, 1992), June 12.
[3] Andrew Murray, *Absolute Surrender* (Moody Publishers, 1988), p. 115.
[4] Ellen Schuknecht and Erin MacPherson, *Free to Parent*, (Family Wings, LCC, 2014), p. 12.
[5] Christine Gross-Loh, "Have American Parents God it All Backwards?" *huffingtonpost.com*, 23 January 2014, www.huffingtonpost.com/christine-grossloh/have-american-parents-got-it-all-backwards_b_3202328.html (accessed 26 July 2015)
[6] Salman Khan, "The Learning Myth: Why I'll Never Tell My Son He's Smart," *huffingtonpost.com*, 19 August 2014, www.huffingtonpost.com/salman-khan/the-learning-myth-why-ill_b_5691681.html (accessed 26 July 2015)
[7] Dr. Carol Dweck, *Mindset: The New Psychology of* (Balantine Books, 2006), pp. 6-7.
[8] Walker Moore, *Escape the Lie* (Randall House, 2014), p. 7.
[9] Oswald Chambers, *My Utmost for His Highest* (Discovery House Publisher, 1992), May 16.
[10] Christine Gross-Loh, *op. cit.*
[11] Elizabeth Huebeck, "Boost Your Health With a Dose of Gratitude: If you want to get healthier, give thanks," *webmd.com*, WebMD Archive, www.webmd.com/women/features/gratitude-health-boost (accessed 26 July 2015)
[12] Anonymous, *Don'ts for Mothers - 1878* (A. & C. Black, Ltd., London)

Dear Reader,

Thank you for taking the time to read "Free to Parent" and to complete this partner workbook. I have prayed diligently that this book would reach parents, teachers, and students in a way that helps them to truly be free in Christ.

Of course, freedom in Christ is a journey, and not a destination. And I would like to continue this journey with you.

- I love hearing stories of transformation, hope, and change! Please drop by my website www.familywings.org and share with me how you have found freedom and hope this year.
- Sign up for my newsletter (find the sign-up on my website) and be the first to know about new books (yes, we have more ideas cooking!), new programs, and new initiatives.
- I do school development and family ministries consulting and would happy to discuss a package with you. Click on the "consulting" page of my site to learn more.
- I also do private parent coaching both in person and via Skype. Contact me for more details.
- If you would like to connect with my daughter and co-author, Erin, her books, blog, and more can be found at www.erinmacpherson.com.

Thank you again, for reading. I look forward to connecting with you more.

In Him,

Ellen

About Ellen Schuknecht

Ellen Schuknecht has been working as an educator for more than 35 years, with experience ranging from early childhood education, to high school advising, to family ministries counseling. Her heart is to minister to young families in a way that's real, doable, and helps them find true joy in their life stage.

She has been married to Glen for almost 40 years and lives nearby her three grown children and her eleven grandchildren. She blogs at www.familywings.org.

Other Books by These Authors

Books by Ellen Schuknecht and Erin MacPherson:

Free to Parent (Family Wings, 2014)

Books by Erin MacPherson:

Hot Mama (Erin MacPherson and Kathi Lipp, Revell, 2015)

The Christian Mama's Guide to Having a Baby (Erin MacPherson, Harper Collins, 2013)

The Christian Mama's Guide to Baby's First Year (Erin MacPherson, Harper Collins, 2013)

The Christian Mama's Guide to Parenting a Toddler (Erin MacPherson, Harper Collins, 2013)

The Christian Mama's Guide to the First School Years (Erin MacPherson, Harper Collins, 2013)

Books Erin and/or Ellen have contributed to:

I Need Some Help Here! Prayers for When Your Kids Don't Go According to Plan (Kathi Lipp, Revell, 2014)

Praying God's Word for Your Life (Kathi Lipp, Revell, 2013)

Praying God's Word for Your Husband (Kathi Lipp, Revell, 2012)

21 Ways to Connect With Your Kids (Kathi Lipp, Harvest House, 2012)

Daily Guideposts 2012, 2013, 2014, 2015, and 2016

Daily Guideposts for New Moms (2011)

Made in the USA
Charleston, SC
26 August 2015